Genetically Modified Foods

TITLES IN THIS SERIES INCLUDE:

Childhood Obesity

Diet and Disease

Food Allergies

Food Myths and Facts

Food Regulation and Safety

Genetically Modified Foods

Junk Food Junkies

Vaccinations

Vegetarianism

NUTRITION & HEALTH

Genetically Modified Foods

KEVIN HILLSTROM

LUCENT BOOKS

A part of Gale, Cengage Learning

GALE
CENGAGE Learning·

Detroit • New York • San Francisco • New Haven, Conn • Waterville, Maine • London

LIBRARY OF CONGRESS CATALOGING-IN-PUBLICATION DATA

Hillstrom, Kevin, 1963-
 Genetically modified foods / by Kevin Hillstrom.
   p. cm. -- (Nutrition and health)
 ISBN 978-1-4205-0722-5 (hardcover)
 1. Genetically modified foods. 2. Food--Biotechnology. I. Title. II. Series:
Nutrition & health (Lucent Books)
 TP248.65.F66H55 2012
 664--dc23

2012002276

Lucent Books
27500 Drake Rd.
Farmington Hills, MI 48331

ISBN-13: 978-1-4205-0722-5
ISBN-10: 1-4205-0722-2

Printed in the United States of America
1 2 3 4 5 6 7 16 15 14 13 12

TABLE OF CONTENTS

Foreword   6

Introduction
The World of Genetically Modified Foods   8

Chapter 1
The Development of Genetically Modified Crops   11

Chapter 2
How Genetically Modified Foods Are Made   26

Chapter 3
The Advantages of Genetically Modified Foods   38

Chapter 4
Concerns About Genetically Modified Foods   51

Chapter 5
The Future of Genetically Modified Crops and
Other Foods   67

Notes   80
Glossary   84
Organizations to Contact   85
For More Information   88
Index   90
Picture Credits   95
About the Author   96

Many people today are often amazed by the amount of nutrition and health information, often contradictory, that can be found in the media. Television, newspapers, and magazines bombard readers with the latest news and recommendations. Television news programs report on recent scientific studies. The healthy living sections of newspapers and magazines offer information and advice. In addition, electronic media such as websites, blogs, and forums post daily nutrition and health news and recommendations.

This constant stream of information can be confusing. The science behind nutrition and health is constantly evolving. Current research often leads to new ideas and insights. Many times, the latest nutrition studies and health recommendations contradict previous studies or traditional health advice. When the media reports these changes without giving context or explanations, consumers become confused. In a survey by the National Health Council, for example, 68 percent of participants agreed that "when reporting medical and health news, the media often contradict themselves, so I don't know what to believe." In addition, the Food Marketing Institute reported that eight out of ten consumers thought it was likely that nutrition and health experts would have a completely different idea about what foods are healthy within five years. With so much contradictory information, people have difficulty deciding how to apply nutrition and health recommendations to their lives. Students find it difficult to find relevant, yet clear and credible information for reports.

Changing recommendations for antioxidant supplements are an example of how confusion can arise. In the 1990s antioxidants such as vitamins C and E and beta-carotene came to the public's attention. Scientists found that people who ate more antioxidant-rich foods had a lower risk of heart disease, cancer, vision loss, and other chronic conditions than those who ate lower amounts. Without waiting for more scientific study, the media and supplement companies quickly spread the word that antioxidants could help fight and prevent disease. They recommended that people take antioxidant supplements and eat fortified foods. When further scientific studies were completed, however, most did not support the initial recommendations. While naturally occurring antioxidants in fruits and vegetables may help prevent a variety of chronic diseases, little scientific evidence proved antioxidant supplements had the same effect. In fact, a study published in the November 2008 *Journal of the American Medical Association* found that supplemental vitamins A and C gave no more heart protection than a placebo. The study's results contradicted the widely publicized recommendation, leading to consumer confusion. This example highlights the importance of context for evaluating nutrition and health news. Understanding a topic's scientific background, interpreting a study's findings, and evaluating news sources are critical skills that help reduce confusion.

Lucent's Nutrition and Health series is designed to help young people sift through the mountain of confusing facts, opinions, and recommendations. Each book contains the most recent up-to-date information, synthesized and written so that students can understand and think critically about nutrition and health issues. Each volume of the series provides a balanced overview of today's hot-button nutrition and health issues while presenting the latest scientific findings and a discussion of issues surrounding the topic. The series provides young people with tools for evaluating conflicting and ever-changing ideas about nutrition and health. Clear narrative peppered with personal anecdotes, fully documented primary and secondary source quotes, informative sidebars, fact boxes, and statistics are all used to help readers understand these topics and how they affect their bodies and their lives. Each volume includes information about changes in trends over time, political controversies, and international perspectives. Full-color photographs and charts enhance all volumes in the series. The Nutrition and Health series is a valuable resource for young people to understand current topics and make informed choices for themselves.

The World of Genetically Modified Foods

Genetically modified (GM) foods are plants and animals that have had their genetic makeup artificially altered by scientists to make them grow faster, taste better, provide more nutrients, or last longer. Scientists make these alterations by transferring genes (also known as DNA) from one organism—plants, trees, fish, animals, bacteria— into another in order to change the condition or character of the receiving organism. This process is known as biotechnology or genetic engineering (GE), and it has revolutionized the way that agriculture is practiced in many parts of the world. Researchers are now able to use GE technology to create "better" versions of milk, tomatoes, alfalfa, corn, soybeans, and other food products that have been consumed by humans for centuries.

As GE technology has developed over the last quarter century, GM foods have become a major part of the diet of most Americans. They are present in the fruit and vegetable bins of grocery stores, as well as in breakfast cereals and many other packaged food items. Yet millions of Americans—both children and adults—are unaware that they are probably eating GM foods every day. When GM crops and products were first approved for sale to the public in the mid-1990s, the federal government declared that they were so hard to tell apart from "regular" food that they did not have to be labeled as genetically modified. Since that time, opponents of GM food have repeatedly urged the U.S. government to require GM labeling so that consumers can decide for themselves whether to purchase such products. Their calls have been unsuccessful. So far, GM foods have expanded to account for a greater and greater percentage of the U.S.—and world—food supply with each passing year.

Many people who *are* aware that they are eating foods created from scientific gene-splicing and other state-of-the-art biotechnology have only the foggiest notion of what genetic modification even means—or whether it is a good thing. Are GM foods safe to eat, or do they pose a potential health threat? Are GM crops good for the environment, or could they wreck fragile ecosystems? Will GM technology help developing nations meet the nutritional needs of malnourished and hungry families, or will it put poor farmers

American grocery shoppers are largely unaware that much of the packaged foods and produce that they eat contains genetically modified ingredients.

at the mercy of corporations that have taken a lead role in developing this new technology? Does genetic modification of our food supply represent a proud new chapter in humankind's quest for knowledge, or is it a sign of disrespect for the natural world—or even of God? Are critics of genetically modified crops, livestock, and fish right to call such creations "Frankenfoods," like the Frankenstein monster of legend? Or do people who throw the term "Frankenfood" around just not recognize how wonderful this technology could be in reducing hunger, combating disease, and limiting environmental damage from farming?

All of these questions are being furiously debated by scientists, environmentalists, religious scholars, public health experts, and parents all around the world. In some places, like western Europe, the attitudes toward GM foods have been generally negative. In others, such as the United States, the technology has been more widely accepted. But the GM debate remains a heated one in both of these regions, as well as in Asia, Latin America, Africa, and other parts of the world. In all of these locations, some people see genetically modified foods as an amazing technological gift for relieving suffering—while many others see the rise of genetically modified foods as an event that could have horrifying long-term consequences for human health and the planet.

The Development of Genetically Modified Crops

O n a Saturday morning in Long Island, New York, two parents—one a mother of three, the other a father of two—discussed their views of genetically modified (GM) foods. The mother, named Sarah, dismissed GM fruits, vegetables, and grains as "Frankenfood" and vowed that she would "absolutely never" buy GM foods for her kids to eat. The father, named Ted, had an entirely different attitude. He said that he had no idea whether the items he was tossing in his grocery cart included GM products, but he was unconcerned. "Everything is going to kill you someday," he said. "If we listened to every last warning or what have you, we'd all starve to death."[1]

The attitudes displayed by Ted and Sarah toward GM foods—also sometimes called transgenic foods—are very different. As journalist Jaclyn Gallucci observed, though, the two parents are similar in one important respect: They began their families in the 1990s, when genetically modified organisms (GMOs) first entered the commercial food supply of the United States. "Sarah and Ted are raising the first generation of genetically modified kids," wrote Gallucci, "and what their future holds is a mystery, a tragedy, or nothing to worry about—depending on whom you ask."[2]

The Development of Genetically Modified Crops 11

Genetic Modification in the Natural World

Although genetically modified foods created in the laboratory are a controversial subject today, genetic modification has actually long been a part of the worlds of both nature and agriculture. "Plants (and animals) genetically modify themselves all the time," observed the PBS science program *NOVA*.

> That's the basis of evolution. We've been genetically modifying plants (and animals) for millennia. That's the basis of agriculture. Our manipulation of a single mustard species has generated such diverse vegetables as broccoli, Brussels sprouts, and cabbage. Altogether, the wild ancestors of grapes, potatoes, and all other fruits and vegetables you find today on grocery-store shelves are but pale shadows of their modern, highly modified descendants. All have gone through countless generations of careful hybridization and genetic breeding to improve yields, taste, size, texture, and other attributes.[3]

Farmers have been selecting and cross-breeding seeds, plants, and animals for thousands of years to improve the quality of their crops and livestock. More than ten thousand years ago, for example, farmers in ancient Mesopotamia mixed cultivated and wild species of wheat to create a hybrid seed that became the ancestor of the wheat we use to make bread today. These conventional breeding methods were slow, however. It took years, decades, or even centuries of continual effort by farmers or ranchers before the traits they were seeking—higher yields from seeds, more beef from cows, great pulling capacity of plow horses, and so on—began to appear. They persevered, though, and over time they managed to

improve the quality of numerous types of crops and species of domestic livestock. Crop and livestock breeding practices continued to advance during the nineteenth century, as farming expanded across much of the North American continent.

An even greater factor, though, was the scientific work of two men—English naturalist Charles Darwin (1809–1882) and Austrian monk Gregor Mendel (1822–1884). Darwin remains best known today for his trailblazing theories about the evolution of humans. However, his observations about "natural selection" also were very important for agriculture. Darwin believed that the strongest and most adaptable organisms of any species had the best chance of surviving in their environment—and of passing on their positive genetic traits to future generations. This theory provided guidance to farmers who wanted to remove undesirable traits or strengthen desirable traits in their crops.

Mendel, meanwhile, conducted so many important breeding experiments with peas that he is sometimes called the father of modern genetics. Working in a monastery garden filled with twenty-nine thousand carefully tended pea plants, Mendel made important breakthroughs in understanding the nature of dominant and recessive genes. As journalist Eoin O'Carroll explained, Mendel observed that the plants'

A relief depicts workers tending to crops in ancient Mesopotamia, where farmers created a hybrid species of wheat thousands of years ago.

The Father of Genetics

Famed geneticist Gregor Johann Mendel was born on July 22, 1822, in a small village in Czechoslovakia. The son of peasants, Mendel worked as a gardener and studied beekeeping before entering the priesthood. In the mid-1840s he took up residence at the Abbey of St. Thomas, a monastery in Brunn, Czechoslovakia. In 1868 he was appointed the chief priest, or abbot, of the monastery.

Mendel lived most of his adult life at the abbey, where his fascination with the natural world led him to pursue all sorts of scientific experiments. He designed his own beehives, for example, and he was an enthusiastic student of both astronomy and meteorology. It was his research with pea plants, though, that made him a legendary figure in the development of modern-day genetics.

Mendel was intrigued by how animals, plants, trees, and other living creatures passed on their characteristics from generation to generation. Using the abbey's gardens as his laboratory, Mendel planted thousands of pea plants and conducted experiments to see how coloration and other plant traits were passed down. His experiments, which unfolded over the course of many years, helped later generations of researchers understand the principles of heredity. Most notably, Mendel proved that different traits did not "blend" together when they were passed down. Rather, these traits were either passed on intact (in the case of dominant genes) or failed to pass on at all (in the case of recessive genes).

When Mendel died on January 6, 1884, from kidney disease, he was remembered by mourners as a teacher and abbot, not as one of the greatest scientists of his day. In the early twentieth century, however, his trailblazing work was discovered by a new generation of scientists. They confirmed his findings and used his insights to gain greater understanding of the laws of inheritance than ever before. As a result, Mendel is commonly referred to today as the father of modern genetics.

Gregor Mendel's work with pea plants provided the basis for modern-day genetics.

traits did not blend together: a pea plant with yellow pods cross-pollinated with one with green pods . . . did not result in [a plant with] yellowish-green pods, as would have been expected. Instead, every single pea in the first generation crop remained yellow."[4] Mendel then self-pollinated the crop and found that while some plants in the second generation went back to being green, most of them remained yellow. Mendel realized at that point that inherited traits remained intact through generations. He said that these traits were carried by "factors," which are known today as genes.

The Age of Agribusiness

By the early twentieth century, seed breeding programs were a widely accepted part of American agriculture. Growers worked hard at creating "hybrid seeds"—seeds created from the union of two other varieties of seeds. Hybrid seeds lifted the production of corn, wheat, and other crops to new heights, and farmers quickly recognized that hybrids were the wave of the future. During the 1920s and 1930s, though, an important change took place in crop breeding practices. Farmers stopped breeding hybrid seeds themselves. Instead they became dependent on buying these seeds from corporations that could devote all of their time, energy, and resources to creating high-yield seeds.

This shift in seed development practices made American agriculture more efficient. Under this new division of responsibilities, everyone in the world of agribusiness— the collective name for all the different sectors of the food industry—could focus on what they did best. Seed companies worked at developing new varieties of fast-growing, high-yield seeds, while farmers spent their time planting, tending, and harvesting the crops that grew out of these seeds. This arrangement, though, also gave large seed corporations significant influence over American farming. The new system, wrote scholar Mark L. Winston,

> changed farming from a simple occupation to an industry and severely reduced the number of varieties being produced for commercial agriculture. In the United States, for example, 786 corn varieties were

available in 1903, but only 52 in 1983, a decrease of 93 percent. Thus farmers who became used to purchasing the latest hybrid variety from their favored seed company each spring were ideally predisposed to accept transgenic corn when those varieties became the corn of choice recommended by seed companies in the mid-1990s.[5]

These changes to American farming took place at the same time that scientists were making important new discoveries about the building blocks of life. In 1953 researchers James Watson and Francis Crick announced their stunning discovery that DNA was shaped like a double helix—a

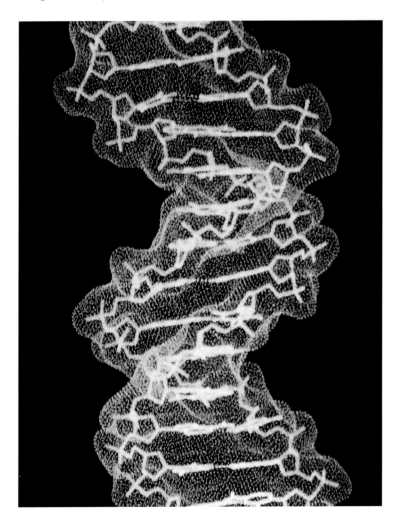

A DNA model shows its form as a double helix, the discovery of which prompted researchers to explore ways to experiment with the genetic modification of organisms.

three-dimensional spiraling ladder. This breakthrough gave scientists a much better understanding of how genetic information was passed from generation to generation in all life forms. In addition, it opened a whole new field of research for geneticists. After Watson and Crick told the world about their discovery, researchers began exploring ways to combine DNA from two different organisms to form a whole new "genetically modified" creation.

America's big agricultural seed and chemical companies leaped to the forefront of this genetic engineering research. They recognized that genetic modification had the potential to create stronger, sturdier, and tastier foods than ever before—and in a fraction of the time that traditional crop breeding programs required. They also realized that genetic engineering could revolutionize meat and dairy production. If researchers could combine the DNA of one of the larger species of cow with one that was known for high-quality and tasty beef, for example, the result had the potential to be highly profitable.

An Important Supreme Court Ruling

As corporations developed new plant hybrids—some through genetic engineering and some through conventional breeding methods—they pushed Congress to grant them patents on the new seeds. A patent is a special privilege granted by the government to inventors and creators of new products. It gives them the sole right to produce and sell the new creation for a set period of time. Congress refused to go along with the corporations' demands for many years, but in 1970 it passed the Plant Variety Protection Act (PVPA).

This legislation gave breeders of crops and other plants (like flowers) the option to obtain a Certificate of Protection (COP) for their new plants. The COP was not a patent, but it did give breeders more control over the use and sale of their plants.

The next big change in Washington related to GM seeds came in 1980. At that time the U.S. Supreme Court narrowly ruled (by a 5–4 vote) that "live human-made microorganisms" were subject to U.S. patent law. Makers of GM seeds recognized that this decision (which came in a case known as *Diamond v. Chakrabarty*) paved the way for the patenting of GM seeds, plants, and other foods. Large agribusiness companies responded by pouring even more money into transgenic research.

GM Foods Arrive in U.S. Grocery Stores

The quest to develop genetically modified foods took on even more urgency in May 1992, when the U.S. government gave its seal of approval to the commercial sale of GM foods and beverages. This approval came from the U.S. Food and Drug Administration (FDA), the federal agency that has primary responsibility for ensuring the safety of America's food supply. The ruling was tremendously encouraging to biotechnology corporations. It assured them that the FDA would not stand in the way of their efforts to create profitable new GM foods.

Eighteen months later, the FDA approved the use of a special growth hormone for dairy cows that had been developed by Monsanto, one of the nation's biggest producers of crop seeds, pesticides, and other farming products. This hormone, known as rBGH (recombinant bovine growth hormone), was a genetically engineered version of the growth hormone naturally produced by cows. It was designed by Monsanto scientists to make dairy cows produce greater quantities of milk.

When FDA commissioner David Kessler announced his agency's decision to approve the commercial sale of GM milk beginning in 1994, he also indicated that milk produced by cows treated with the hormone would not have to be specially labeled. "There is virtually no difference in milk from treated and untreated cows," he explained. "In fact, it's not possible using current scientific techniques to tell them apart. We have looked carefully at every single question raised, and we are confident this product is safe for consumers, for cows, and for the environment."[6] The labeling decision horrified consumer advocates, environmental activists, and ordinary parents who were already upset about the FDA's approval of GM technology. How could they possibly tell which foods were bioengineered and which ones were raised through traditional methods if their labels were identical?

GM Labels and Informed Consumers

One of the most frequent complaints about GM foods in the United States and Canada is that they are not labeled. Mickie, a teenager who lives in Hamilton, Ontario, Canada, believes that this state of affairs is extremely unfair to consumers. "GM foods should be a CHOICE for us, but only a choice," she said.

Science has made some amazing leaps through genetic modification that I think will prove to be good for us as time goes on. Plus I have been exposed to GM foods my entire life. Eating them has been a daily occurrence. Maybe it would be a different story if I had never been exposed to this kind of product. But in my fourteen years there has not been any major side effect that I am aware of. I am healthy and do not feel that GM foods have restricted my abilities at all. Nevertheless, . . . there should always be a choice. If GM foods are to stay on the market they must be labeled so that consumers can decide for themselves what they want to be putting into their mouths and their families' mouths.

"Genetically Modified Foods: Disaster or Delight?" n.d. TeenInk.com. www.teenink.com/opinion/current _events_politics/article/181484/Genetically-Modified -Foods-Disaster-or-Delight/.

Labels that indicate that a food product contains GM ingredients are not required in the United States and Canada.

Their protests, however, failed to halt the march of GM foods into American grocery stores. In 1994 FDA officials approved the commercial sale of the FlavrSavr tomato, which had been genetically modified to slow its ripening process. The tomato's creator, a California-based biotechnology company called Calgene, hoped that the longer-lasting tomato would be a hit with consumers. Despite claims that it tasted even better than "ordinary" tomatoes, though, the FlavrSavr

Activists in New York City protest against the use of rBGH in dairy cows in 1994, after the FDA approved the sale of GM milk.

tomato campaign was a disaster. Calgene proved to be so unfamiliar with the basics of growing, marketing, and transporting tomatoes of *any* kind that its FlavrSavr operation was suspended after only a few months.

The problem, wrote science reporter Daniel Charles, was that Calgene's "Flavr Savr gene . . . simply didn't make tomatoes noticeably better. Far more important than the new gene were the basics of the business: the varieties you grew and the way you handled the tomatoes, sorted them, and marketed them. The company would have done just as well—or just as badly—growing vine-ripened tomatoes that weren't genetically engineered."[7] Calgene never really recovered from this failure. In 1997 Monsanto, which had grand ambitions to transform itself into the "Microsoft of agriculture," purchased the company and all of its GM research and products.

GM Products Transform America's Food Industry

Despite the FlavrSavr flop, America's food industry expressed enormous excitement about GM technology and its potential to bring about a new era of higher crop yields, tastier fruits, and more nutritious vegetables. Food biotechnology companies were not the only ones who harbored big dreams about "superfoods," either. In fact, many crop growers and livestock owners were impatient to get their hands on GM seeds and hormones. As Charles wrote

> America's farm country [became full of] rumors of savior genes and miracle crops that weren't yet legal to plant. A few genetically engineered plants already were in the fields, to be sure [in the mid-1990s]. In addition to Calgene's ill-fated tomato, Asgrow [seed company now owned by Monsanto] was selling seed for squash plants that were resistant to viruses, farmers in Georgia were growing Calgene's genetically engineered canola plants, producing oil suitable for use in soaps and detergents, and Monsanto had begun selling [genetically modified] potatoes. But these crops covered only a few thousand acres. . . . They were mere ripples in the ocean; a tsunami [tidal wave] was approaching.[8]

The tsunami hit the United States in a succession of waves in the late 1990s and early 2000s. The FDA gave its stamp of approval to all sorts of GM foods during this time, and farmers and food processors were quick to take advantage. By 2001 genetically modified varieties of corn accounted for 26 percent of the U.S. crop, while 68 percent of the soybeans planted in American fields that year were GM. Nearly 70 percent of U.S. cotton production—the source of cottonseed oil used in animal feed—also came from GM crops that year. This first generation of GM crops shared several common characteristics. Nearly all were designed to produce higher yields than their conventional counterparts. They also were crafted so that they were more resistant to pesticides—chemicals applied to kill bugs or weeds.[9]

In 2002 the U.S. Supreme Court explicitly ruled that patents could be granted for GM seeds and other foods. This decision gave big corporations even more incentive to develop herbicide-resistant seeds. Monsanto, for instance, developed and patented GM seeds that were resistant to the company's own herbicide, which it called Roundup. This arrangement enabled Monsanto to make money selling both GM seeds and herbicide for farmers' fields.

By 2003—only seven years after farmers began planting GM corn, soybeans, and cotton for commercial use—the U.S. Department of Agriculture estimated that as much as 75 percent of all the processed foods available in the United States contained GM ingredients. This astounding growth reflected the fact that the American food biotechnology industry was pouring billions of dollars into GM research. In addition, it showed how quickly big companies like Monsanto were able to convince farmers, dairy owners, and livestock breeders that bioengineered foods—which only a few years earlier had seemed like something out of a science fiction tale—were essential to their future prosperity.

Even so, there were some problems along the way. In glaring contrast to the United States, a number of major food markets around the world declared that they wanted nothing to do with GM foods. Countries like Japan and New Zealand passed laws forbidding the sale of GM foods, as did the European Union (EU). Anti-GM sentiment in

A harvester makes its way through a field of GM corn on a California farm in the the first years of the twenty-first century, the decade in which GM technology came to dominate commercial crop production in the United States.

the EU, which contained twenty-seven nations in 2011, has been particularly strong over the years. In 1999 many EU members took firm stands against the sale of GM crops and products derived from them, and GM advocates have not had much success in removing these barriers.

In the United States, meanwhile, occasional news stories have fanned controversy about the technology. In the fall of 2000, for example, health authorities discovered that a genetically engineered strain of corn that had only been approved for use as livestock feed had become mixed up in America's human food supply. The discovery that so-called StarLink corn had found its way into Taco Bell brand taco

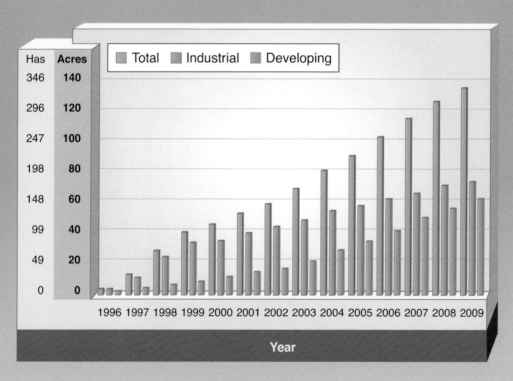

Global Area of GM Crops, 1996 to 2009: Industrial and Developing Countries
(Millions of Hectares [Has] and Millions of Acres)

Taken from: Clive James, 2010. http://cspinet.org/new/pdf/infocus-summer10.pdf.

shells was upsetting to many American consumers and food safety advocates. They claimed that the incident showed that the nation's food safety laws and regulations were not strong enough to keep GM products from contaminating non-GM foods.

Despite such missteps, however, U.S. farmers planted greater volumes of genetically modified crops with each passing year. By 2007 GM crops were growing on 57.7 million hectares (142.6 million acres) of American farmland. This shift toward GM crops was so great that the United States alone accounted for more than half of all global GM food production. More than two dozen other countries support some GM food production, though, including fast-growing nations like Argentina, Brazil, China, and India.

By 2008, in fact, eight countries (the United States, Argentina, Brazil, India, Canada, China, Paraguay, and South Africa) accounted for 98 percent of the 125 million hectares (308 million acres) of land devoted to GM crop production. Of this total, 57 percent of GM croplands were located in North America, 32 percent in Latin America, 6 percent in India, and 3 percent in China.

CHAPTER 2

How Genetically Modified Foods Are Made

Bioengineered foods are created by manipulating DNA (deoxyribonucleic acid), the molecules that are the building blocks of all life. DNA is the material that makes up genes, which in turn determine your physical appearance, your intelligence, and other aspects of your being. Each cell in the human body contains somewhere in the range of twenty-five thousand to thirty-five thousand genes, each of which has been shaped and passed down by your parents in the form of traits. "For example," notes the website KidsHealth, "if both of your parents have green eyes, you might inherit the trait of green eyes from them. Or if your mom has freckles, you might inherit that trait and wind up with a freckled face. And genes aren't just in humans—*all* animals and plants have genes, too."[10]

Prying Open the Secrets of DNA

In 1953 scientists James Watson and Francis Crick announced that they had discovered the basic structure of DNA. Their breakthrough opened the door for scientists to learn much more about how genetic information was passed down through generations. Researchers also gained a much greater understanding of how individual genes are organized.

They discovered, for example, that genes are bundled into chromosomes, which serve as packaging for all the genetic information that gets passed down during reproduction.

Over time, scientists learned how to identify and isolate genes that carried the blueprints for specific characteristics in humans, animals, and plants. These genes provide instructions for the development of all sorts of traits in life forms, including size, shape, length, strength, color, and health. By the 1970s scientists had learned so much about DNA, chromosomes, and genes that they could take a specific gene from one plant or animal and insert it into another

A laboratory technician oversees containers of GM fruit trees. Experiments with transgenics have allowed scientists to create new and better versions of existing plants and animals.

one. "Since the DNA code is essentially universal," wrote food safety advocates Warren Leon and Caroline Smith DeWaal, "the transferred gene can often function in the new organism in which it is placed. Although the methods of genetic engineering were initially laborious and limiting, both scientists and financial investors understood the long-term potential of the technology. Billions of dollars were quickly invested in biotechnology companies."[11]

As research into bioengineering intensified, scientists learned not only how to transfer genes from one type of organism into the same type of organism, but also how to move genes from one organism into an entirely different kind of organism. Plants, animals, and bacteria that undergo these sorts of transformations became known as genetically modified organisms (GMOs) or transgenic organisms, and the transferred genes were called transgenes. The practice itself, meanwhile, became known as genetic engineering, bioengineering, or genetic modification.

This remarkable innovation led to all sorts of experiments to create new and better versions of existing plants and animals, from pest-resistant sugar beets to meatier hogs. "A gene can be taken from a broccoli plant or bacterium and inserted into a potato plant to make a new, genetically modified type of potato," affirmed Leon and DeWaal. "Even more dramatically, a fish or a fox gene can be inserted into a lettuce plant."[12]

These options marked a big change from conventional breeding methods. "Traditional breeders were bound by the restraints of biology, while modern genetic engineers are in theory bound only by the laws of physics, by their imagination, and by the laws and ethics of their society,"[13] observed scientists Ian Wilmut and Keith Campbell, who carried out the first successful cloning of a sheep in 1996. Scientists seemed to become more creative and imaginative with each passing year. To create more frost-resistant strawberries, for example, researchers began introducing the genes that kept Arctic species of fish from freezing in cold, icy waters. Similarly fanciful experiments continue to take place today in bioengineering laboratories all around the world.

Three Types of GM Breeding Methods

In the years since scientists first began unlocking the secrets of DNA and creating GM foods, three main methods of breeding have been utilized. The first of these is known as *tissue culture,* and it involves growing whole plants from single cells or plant cultures nurtured in the laboratory—rather than from seeds raised in soil.

Another option available to biotechnologists is *anther culture.* Under this procedure, breeders focus on the anther section of the stamen—the male reproductive part of flowers and plants. Anthers contain pollen, which are the male cells for reproduction. Breeders select pollen to produce new varieties of plants with special traits. Anther culture has been used in more than two hundred species, including foods (such as tomato, rice, and barley) and decorative flowers (such as geranium).

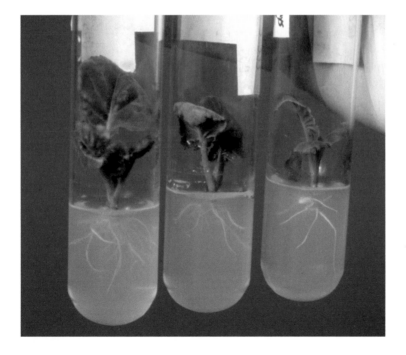

Cauliflower grown from tissue culture grows in laboratory test tubes. Tissue culture allows whole plants to be grown without seeds.

Using DNA to Predict a Child's Athletic Future

Scientific knowledge about DNA, cells, and other building blocks of life have enabled us to make big changes in the way that we raise our food and treat diseases. This technology, though, is also being harnessed for a variety of other purposes. In Colorado, for example, a company called Atlas Sports Genetics says that it has developed a procedure to predict the athletic future of children using DNA analysis. Parents simply swab inside their child's mouth to collect DNA and send it to Atlas to analyze the characteristics of a gene known as ACTN3. According to Atlas, studies indicate that different variants, or types, of ACTN3 make children better at different kinds of sports. One variant, for example, might make a kid better at endurance sports like swimming or cross-country running, while another might suggest that the child would excel at power sports like football or wrestling.

Some parents have jumped to take advantage of this testing. "I could see how some people might think the test would pigeonhole your child into doing fewer sports or being exposed to fewer things, but I still think it's good to match them with the right activity," said one Colorado mother. A father of two in Minnesota

Atlas Sports Genetics claims a child's DNA can be used to determine an ability to excel at an endurance sport such as swimming.

agreed. "I'm a pretty open-minded kind of guy and keep all doors open because you never know which one can give you education that can help your kids go into a direction that gives them confidence. Not just in sports, but in life."

Some genetics experts, however, have expressed reservations about the test. Dr. Stephen M. Roth, for example, told the *New York Times* that athletic performance is affected by at least two hundred genes. "The idea that it will be one or two genes that are contributing to the [Olympic swimmer] Michael Phelpses or the [Olympic sprinter] Usain Bolts of the world I think is shortsighted because it's much more complex than that," he said.

"DNA Swab Tests Kids' Athletic Ability." NECN.com, November 13, 2011. www.necn.com/11/13/11/DNA -swab-tests-kids-athletic-ability/landing.html?blockID =593222&feedID=4213.

Juliet Macur. "Born to Run? Little Ones Get Test for Sports Gene." *New York Times*, November 29, 2008. www.nytimes.com/2008/11/30/sports/30genetics.html ?pagewanted=all.

Gene marker selection is the third GM breeding method. This procedure for creating GM food involves "linking a molecular DNA 'tag' to the genes on the chromosome that govern a special trait you want to breed into a new variety," explained journalist Peter Pringle. "Once the genes governing a trait have been linked to a DNA 'tag,' the desired trait can be moved by traditional cross-breeding to the new variety—and the 'tag' shows the new trait is present."[14]

Techniques for Gene Transference

Scientists have employed a number of techniques over the years for transferring genes from host organisms into receiving or recipient organisms. Like genetic modification as a whole, many of these techniques seem as if they were pulled directly out of a science fiction movie or a futuristic comic book. They are real, though—and they are used every day in bioengineering research laboratories around the world.

Viral and Bacterial Carriers. The oldest transgenic techniques use viruses or bacteria as carriers to deliver foreign DNA into targeted plants and animals. This approach is sometimes also known as the recombinant DNA technique. Under the bacterial carrier approach, scientists introduce the genes they want to transfer into a bacterium, then insert the bacterium into the targeted organism. The bacterium thus infects the receiving organism with the new genes. The viral carrier approach is very similar. Viruses are infectious particles that contain genetic material to which a new gene can easily be added. Viruses can thus be used to introduce new genes into recipient organisms. As the virus invades the cells of the receiving organism and replicates—makes duplicate copies of itself—the selected DNA is transferred into the target cells of the receiving organism.

Biolistics. With this technique, scientists take DNA containing desired genes for transference and attach it to microscopic slivers of gold or tungsten, a hard and rare metal. These DNA-coated particles are then shot into the target cells of the receiving organism with a burst of pressurized gas. Once it passes into the interior of the cell, the new genetic material becomes incorporated into the wider

DNA structure of the targeted organism. Scientists sometimes compare this technique, which is also known as particle bombardment and bioballistics, to firing a tiny bullet out of a gene gun. So far this technique is used mostly with plants, but molecular biologists say that it holds promise as an agent for treating human illnesses and frailties and as a method for making genetic changes to livestock and other animals.

Electoporation. This is one of the most sophisticated techniques for genetic modification of crops and other organisms. Under electoporation, targeted cells are bathed in a special liquid solution that contains the DNA that scientists want to transfer. Scientists then use a brief burst of electricity to make small tears in the cell walls. These tears provide the DNA with pathways to enter and transform the targeted cells. Once this step has been concluded, the cells are placed into another solution that prompts them to begin repairing the tears in their walls—with the transferred DNA still inside. Once this repair job has been accomplished, the transferred DNA becomes locked inside the cells and the genetic transfer is complete.

Calcium phosphate precipitation. Under this procedure, DNA that has been selected for transference to another organism is exposed to calcium phosphate, a powdery mineral that is used in everything from plastics and glass to toothpaste and plant fertilizer (it is also a primary ingredient in cow's milk, bones, and tooth enamel). The resulting mixture creates tiny grains that are introduced to target cells in the host organism. The target cells then naturally absorb the grains. When they do so, the DNA that was mixed with the calcium phosphate is released and becomes part of the genetic makeup of the receiving organism.

Lipofection. Molecular biologists engaged in the field of genetic engineering also have the option of using liposomes—essentially small bubbles of fat—as gene carriers. With this process, DNA-carrying liposomes and target cells are placed together in a special liquid solution. Over time, the liposomes

FOOD FACT

The human body is composed of about 200 million cells.

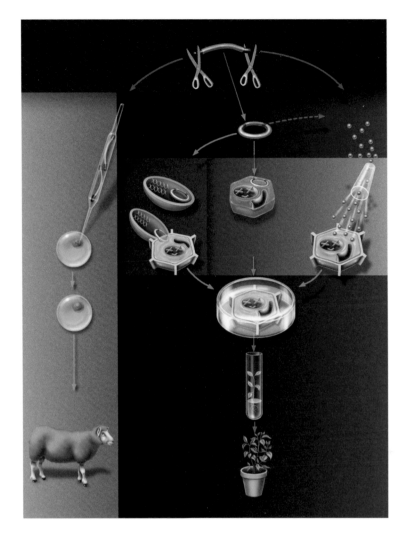

A diagram illustrates several techniques used for transfering genes, including (from left) microinjection, the use of bacterial carriers, electroporation, and biolistics.

(and the genetic material they are carrying) merge into the membranes of the target cells. This is one of the most popular techniques for genetic modification. It is a relatively easy procedure, and it can be used with many different types of organisms.

Microinjection. This is another relatively simple procedure. With this technique, bioengineers simply inject genetic material they want to transfer directly into recipient female egg cells of animals and plants. The main tool they use for this is a slender glass needle. The genetically modified egg cell is then transplanted into the prepared uterus of a receptive female and allowed to grow to term. This method ensures that almost every cell in the developing organism's body will contain the modified DNA.

Gene silencing. Some genetic modification is accomplished by "silencing" genes that have undesirable traits, such as the production of proteins that cause human allergies. Scientists can do this in a variety of different ways, including through the insertion of foreign DNA that stops genes from producing the unwanted proteins.

Gene splicing. In this process, scientists use chemicals called restriction enzymes like scissors to cut foreign DNA chromosome strands apart. They can then paste any genetic modifications they wish onto the broken chain. Once this has been accomplished, they use another enzyme called ligase to fuse the new gene sequences into the chromosome. This technique gives bioengineers the capacity to splice together genetic material from all sorts of animals, plants, and bacteria. Thus far, however, it has been used primarily in the health field to produce insulin and other important medicines.

GM Technology a Source of Distrust?

All of these procedures are testaments to the brilliance and ingenuity of molecular biologists and other scientists around the world. The advances in GM technology that they have made over the past few decades are truly amazing. Looking to the future, these techniques are almost certainly going to become even more sophisticated—and lead us into research directions that we cannot possibly predict now.

In some respects, though, supporters of GM foods and other types of genetic engineering say that the mind-boggling complexity of bioengineering has actually become a problem of sorts. Ordinary people, whether they live in North America, Europe, Asia, Africa, or Latin America, have expressed reservations about genetic engineering in part because it is so beyond their understanding. Journalist Robert Manning recalled, "A young postdoctoral student in a molecular biology lab once told me the problem with her line of work is that she can't explain to her mother what she does."

Bt and HT Genes in GM Crops

Genetically modified versions of corn, cotton, and other major cash crops are currently transformed in two ways. Some GM corn and cotton is known as "Bt," because the plants contain a gene that causes them to produce a bacterial protein called *Bacillus thuringiensis* that is toxic to certain insects. Bt genes do not themselves increase the size of crops, but they are valuable to farmers because their pest-killing properties reduce crop losses from insects such as the cotton-boll weevil and the maize stem borer. Some growers of Bt corn and cotton find that they can reduce their spending on pesticides.

The other main genes that have been introduced into today's crops are HT (herbicide-tolerant) genes. Crops that have been modified through HT genes are extremely tolerant of herbicides. Farmers who plant HT crops can thus make heavier use of weed-killing chemicals without worrying that the chemicals will damage their crops.

In recent years, Monsanto and other big biotechnology companies have increasingly invested in "hybrid seeds" that utilize both Bt and HT genes. These seeds are sometimes described as "stacked," because they have both traits genetically engineered into them.

A farmer in Georgia inspects his crop of Bt cotton.

This is more than a personal problem. If the rest of us ... could get some sort of idea of what is being done in those labs, we would better understand the depth of the world's environmental problems and the character of life itself. Indeed, those scientists who tinker with DNA have drifted into isolation from the rest of us, simply because they see something we cannot.[15]

This distrust is particularly strong in countries where citizens harbor doubts about whether their governments and businesses are ready, willing, and able to protect them from danger. They worry that if their society's guardians fail to fulfill their ethical responsibilities to protect food consumers from harm, their families—and the world itself—may become victims of technology gone crazy. "Genetically

The complexity involved in creating GM foods has led many to be distrustful of their use and concerned about their impact on people's health and the environment.

modified crops have been called a lightning rod for a host of environmental, social, and political concerns," acknowledged one analysis.

> The controversy surrounding these products involves fear of new technology, distrust of government, hostility toward large multinational corporations, anxiety about food safety, concern for the sanctity of life, and even a science-fiction fear of mutant monsters. The issues are as complex as the technology, and the solutions are far from clear.[16]

CHAPTER **3**

The Advantages of Genetically Modified Foods

S upporters of genetically modified (GM) foods argue that they have many far-reaching benefits. They say that GM seeds provide economic help to farmers through increased crop yields and lower expenditures on pesticides. They also claim that the technology has important benefits for consumers, including lower food costs, tastier and more nutritious food, and reduced exposure to disease-causing agents in traditional food sources. Champions of GM technology even claim that bioengineered foods have the potential to reduce—or even end—malnutrition and hunger in poverty-stricken parts of the world.

Besides these health and economic benefits, pro-GM scientists, scholars, policy makers, and consumers believe that transgenic technology could greatly reduce environmental problems associated with traditional farming methods. They claim, for example, that higher yields associated with GM crops will reduce farming pressure on undeveloped wildlife habitat. Another frequently mentioned benefit of GM crops is that they require smaller applications of insecticides and herbicides that sometimes pollute water sources and kill nonthreatening plants and insects. Finally, supporters of GM food technology point out that if biotechnology corporations can develop and sell transgenic versions of salmon and other threatened fish species, those wild fish are less likely to be harvested to extinction.

Keeping People Healthier and Disease-Free

Supporters of genetically engineered foods often voice excitement about the ways in which GM technology could improve the health of hundreds of millions of people around the world. They point out that scientists have already made genetically modified rice, wheat, fruits, and other foods that are more nutritious to eat than their traditionally grown counterparts. GM expert Peter Pringle notes that researchers have even developed a genetically modified soybean that elevates omega-3 acids in the blood. "Found naturally in salmon, trout, and fresh tuna, these fatty acids are known to protect against heart disease and diabetes and to help the growth of

Scientists have developed a GM soybean that elevates blood levels of omega-3 acids, which have many health benefits.

brain cells in the young," according to Pringle. "People may be able to eat soy instead of fish in order to obtain their essential omega-3s. It would be a double benefit—a healthier diet and less stress on fish stocks in our increasingly overfished oceans."[17]

Other GM foods have been designed to carry additional vitamins, while others eliminate unwanted genes—such as those that produce caffeine or trans fats. Genetic engineering can even be used to remove genes associated with food allergies. For example, scientists are working on blocking the gene in peanut plants that makes some people allergic to peanuts.

GM food could also become an effective means for carrying out large-scale vaccinations of thousands or even millions of people. "We are merely at the beginning of a great GM plant revolution, only starting to see the astonishing range of potential applications" of the technology, declared James D. Watson, one of the scientists who discovered the structure of DNA in 1953.

> Apart from delivering nutrients where they are wanting, plants may also one day hold the key to distributing orally administered vaccine proteins. By simply engineering a banana that produces, say, the polio vaccine protein—which would remain intact in the fruit, which travels well and is most often eaten uncooked— we could one day distribute the vaccine to parts of the world that lack public health infrastructure.[18]

A Safe Food Source

People who support GM foods dismiss complaints that they might not be safe to eat. To the contrary, they assert that GM foods are likely to be *more* nutritious and contain *smaller* amounts of pesticide residues than foods raised by traditional farming methods.

Besides, they argue, processed foods and drinks contained "unnatural" chemical ingredients (such as preservatives and food colorings) long before GM technology came along. "And although GM food isn't entirely natural, that isn't necessarily a bad thing," wrote Johnjoe McFadden, a British professor of molecular genetics.

Food poisoning agents such as salmonella are natural, and they kill thousands of people each year. Even plants have got it in for us. Although many have evolved tasty fruits to tempt animals into scattering their seeds, they have no interest in our long-term welfare. Lots of plants produce powerful toxins to deter pests. Crops including beans and cassava [a food

Biotechnology companies maintain that GM strawberries and other foods are heavily tested for safety before they are approved for sale to the public.

grown in tropical countries] produce cyanide that has to be removed before cooking. And of course, many of our most prevalent chronic illnesses in the West—from coronary heart disease to diabetes—are related to our consumption of perfectly normal constituents of our diet, such as fat, sugar or salt. . . . As far as we know, GM food is just as safe (or as dangerous) as conventional food.[19]

Companies engaged in biotechnology research also insist that GM products ranging from milk to strawberries to corn are heavily tested to make sure they are safe to eat and environmentally friendly before they are approved for commercial sale. In addition, industry spokespeople point out that all of the nations that are heavily involved in GM food production maintain rules and regulations governing the production and sale of genetically engineered foods and beverages. In the United States, for example, three different federal agencies—the Environmental Protection Agency (EPA), the U.S. Department of Agriculture (USDA), and the Food and Drug Administration (FDA)—have responsibilities to make sure that GM foods are safe.

Economic Benefits for Farmers and Consumers

Supporters of transgenic foods also claim that the technology can provide economic benefits to both farmers and consumers. They acknowledge that GM seeds are more expensive to purchase than conventional seeds, but they say that farmers who plant GM crops ultimately come out ahead. Since GM seeds generate higher crop yields, farmers bring in more money at harvest time. In addition, they do not have to spend as much money on expensive pesticides since many GM crops have been designed for increased resistance to insects.

GM crops, in other words, can be raised far more efficiently than conventional crops. "We'll soon be able to produce more crops with less pesticide, less fuel, less fertilizer, fewer trips over the field. We'll produce much more with much less," said Dr. Ray Bressan, who serves as the director

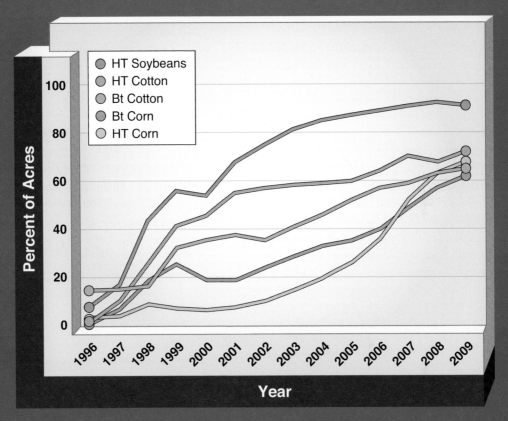

Rapid Growth in Adoption of Genetically Engineered Crops Continues in the United States

Data for each crop category include varieties with both HT and Bt (stacked) traits.
Sources: 1996–1999 data are from Jorge Fernandez-Cornejo and William D.McBride (2002).

Taken from: http://cspinet.org/new/pdf/infocus-summer10.pdf.

of Purdue University's Center for Plant Environmental Stress Physiology. "A couple of years ago I wouldn't have predicted this. But I now think that . . . it will be possible to have crops that can withstand the stresses of early spring and late fall to such an extent that farmers could plant two crops of corn, soybeans, or wheat each year."[20]

One African Researcher's Perspective on GM Foods

In considering whether it is wise for our planet to pursue widespread genetic modification of its food supply, some observers point out that it may depend on where you live. The stakes are different for Americans and other peoples with easy access to food than they are for malnourished peoples in parts of Africa and Asia.

Many communities in the third world are desperate to improve their food security. As a result, some policy makers, scientists, farmers, and food consumers in these parts of the world angrily reject the anti-GM position. Florence Wambugu, for example, is a plant researcher from Kenya who works in the biotechnology industry.

She says that anti-GM protestors are denying Kenya and other developing countries "the resources to develop a technology that can help alleviate hunger, malnutrition and poverty. . . . Biotech is a powerful new tool that can help address some of the agricultural problems that plague Africa. The protestors have fanned the flames of mistrust of genetically modified foods through a campaign of misinformation. . . . I know of what I speak, because I grew up barefoot and hungry."

Florence Wambugu. "Biotechnology: Protestors Don't Grasp Africa's Need." *Los Angeles Times,* November 11, 2001. http://articles.latimes.com/2001/nov/11/opinion/op-2845.

A Kenyan farmer pulls up sprouts from a corn crop that failed because of drought.

Many advocates of GM agriculture claim that as farmers see their operating expenses go down and their profits go up, consumers will see food prices at their local grocery store go down. This is an important consideration for many families who struggle to make ends meet.

Ending Hunger and Malnutrition in the Third World

People who defend GM foods frequently spend a lot of time discussing the technology's potential to reduce hunger and malnutrition in poor nations in Asia, Africa, and Latin America. These "third world" countries, as they are sometimes known, are home to millions of impoverished people who struggle every day to find enough food to sustain themselves and their families. GM advocates say that bioengineered crops and livestock could relieve much of this pain and suffering. They point out that fields planted with GM crops produce more food than conventional farmlands on a per-acre basis. The promise of higher yields means a lot to struggling farming families in these regions of the world. Many of them resent anti-GM arguments made by activists who live in wealthy countries like the United States. "I challenge those who oppose GM crops for emergent [developing] farmers to stand up and deny my fellow farmers and me the benefit of earning this extra income and more than sufficient food for our families," said one South African farmer. A poor farmer from India expressed similar views. Before GM pest-resistant cotton came along, she recalled, "yields were very low and we used to incur losses, so we were perpetually losing money. . . . We were badly off." After two years of planting GM cotton, though, cotton-growing "actually turned profitable."[21]

In addition, GM foods can be packed with vitamins and other healthy nutrients that are lacking in third world diets. GM technology can also help poor

FOOD FACT

In 2009 the Food and Agriculture Organization (FAO) of the United Nations estimated that more than 800 million people around the world do not have enough to eat.

At right in photo, a GM variety of brinjal, a popular vegetable in India, shows no signs of insect damage compared to the non-GM variety on the left. GM advocates maintain that bioengineered food could bring relief to regions affected by hunger and malnutrition.

farmers defend their fields against weeds, insects, and other pests that can damage or destroy non-GM crops. Finally, GM technology has progressed to the point that scientists are developing transgenic crops capable of thriving under environmental conditions (such as cold, drought, or flooding) that would wipe out non-GM plants. Such crops could help poor communities increase the amount of land usable for farming.

Supporters of transgenic foods warn, though, that greater investments in GM seeds and technology need to take place immediately if we hope to avoid widespread famine in places like Africa in the coming decades. Most countries—both wealthy and poor—are experiencing steady growth in their populations, which will increase food demand worldwide. "Helping farmers in developing countries produce

more food without doing damage to natural resources is an essential component of the action needed to reduce existing poverty, hunger and malnutrition and to assure that future generations have access to the food they need at reasonable prices," declared food policy expert Per Pinstrup-Anderson.

> Science must be put to work to develop drought tolerance and pest resistance in crops, higher nutrient quality of staple foods, reduced animal diseases, mitigation of negative climate change effects and a host of other solutions to the current food losses and risks facing farmers and consumers in developing countries. The most appropriate scientific approaches, including genetic engineering and other molecular biology, must be applied.[22]

Protecting Wilderness Habitat and Endangered Species

Supporters of GM foods say that the environment also benefits from transgenic crops. They point out that if foods are engineered so that they require fewer applications of fertilizer, herbicides, and insecticides, then nearby rivers and lakes are less likely to become contaminated with these chemicals. Reduced use of farming chemicals also means reduced levels of pesticide residue on nearby plants and trees that wild creatures rely on for their survival. When China came up with a genetically engineered version of cotton that exuded a natural insecticide, for example, pesticide use on that nation's cotton crop fell by 80 percent. "This is no small matter," wrote journalist Richard Manning. "When cotton farmers in China sprayed each year, they logged a human body count [suffered deaths from chemical exposure]. Certainly environmentalists can be cheered by this."[23]

Finally, some supporters of GM agriculture say that the technology has the potential to become the greatest wilderness conservation program in world history. They say that transgenic seeds can help us to grow greater volumes of food without increasing the amount of land we devote to farming. GM foods can thus protect wild forests and grasslands—and

Genetic Modification Saves Hawaiian Papaya Growers

As GM technology has become more sophisticated, it has been used by scientists on several occasions to help farmers and orchard keepers defend their crops from damaging diseases. In Hawaii, for example, growers of papaya have long feared papaya ringspot virus, which can destroy entire orchards. In the 1950s, in fact, papaya production on the Hawaiian island of Oahu was almost completely wiped out by an outbreak of the disease. The outbreak became so bad that almost all papaya production had to be moved to the larger island of Hawaii, where the virus had not yet shown itself.

Papaya production on Hawaii remained stable until the early 1990s, when growers heard the news they had been dreading for so many years: The papaya ringspot virus had reached Hawaii. By 1995 the virus had spread so much that the state's entire papaya industry was in danger of collapsing. Genetic engineers came to the rescue, though. They figured out a way to expose papaya genes to a very small amount of the virus gene. This gene-splicing process immunized papaya trees against the ringspot virus in much the same way that humans use vaccinations for protection against flu and polio. The scientists then launched an ambitious breeding program to pass this immunity on to papaya orchards across the island. By 2000 most papaya farmers were using the GM seeds, which yielded twenty times more papaya than non-GM papaya plants suffering from the virus. "The story of Hawaiian papayas," wrote Pamela C. Ronald and Raoul W. Adamchak, "is an example where GE was the most appropriate technology to address a specific agricultural problem. There was no other technology then to protect the papaya from this devastating disease, nor is there today."

Pamela C. Ronald and Raoul W. Adamchak. *Tomorrow's Table: Organic Farming Genetics, and the Future of Food.* New York: Oxford University Press, 2008, pp. 58–59.

Fruit hangs from a papaya tree in Hawaii.

the creatures that live within—from development that would shatter their fragile ecosystems.

One of the most influential advocates of this viewpoint was Norman Borlaug, a Nobel Prize–winning agricultural expert. During the 1960s Borlaug had used traditional breeding methods to develop high-yielding varieties of wheat that helped prevent famine in many parts of the world. Borlaug's research triggered a so-called Green Revolution in farming practices across much of the planet. According to Borlaug, the movement he helped launch showed how important it is for people to accept new advances in farming when they come along. "In 1960, the production of the 17 most important food, feed, and fiber crops—virtually all of the important crops grown in the U.S. at that time and still grown today—was 252 million tons," he said.

Chemical fungicides and pesticides are sprayed on a bell pepper crop in Florida. Biotechnology advocates note that GM crops reduce the need for such chemicals, which can have a negative impact on waterways and wildlife.

By 1990, it had more than doubled, to 596 million tons, and was produced on 25 million fewer acres than were cultivated in 1960. If we had tried to produce the harvest of 1990 with the technology of 1960, we would have had to have increased the cultivated area by another 177 million hectares, about 460 million more acres of land of the same quality, which we didn't have. . . . We would have moved into marginal grazing areas and plowed up things that wouldn't be productive in the long run. We would have had to move into rolling mountainous country and chop down our forests.[24]

Many supporters of genetically modified food production argue that the technology has the potential to generate similar wilderness conservation benefits. The key, they say, is for us to set aside our overblown fears and introduce GM crops into parts of the world that will otherwise see their forests converted into fields.

CHAPTER 4

Concerns About Genetically Modified Foods

Although genetically modified (GM) foods have become a big presence in U.S. restaurants, supermarkets, kitchens, and school lunchrooms since the late 1990s, they are still viewed with suspicion by many American consumers. Distrust of GM technology is even greater across much of Europe, which maintains extremely rigid laws limiting the production and sale of transgenic foods.

Opponents of GM farming and food raise a wide range of concerns about the technology. Some express anxiety about the long-term health impact of eating genetically engineered foods—or "Frankenfoods," as critics sometimes call them. Others claim that in our haste to create GM crops and animals, we run the risk of accidentally creating pesticide-resistant weeds and insects that could disrupt delicate ecosystems and damage food supplies. Environmental groups like Greenpeace have also warned that if the genes of GM crops and animals mix with those of traditional plants and wild animals, we might lose some non-GM species forever. Critics have even questioned whether GM technology will make food far more accessible and affordable to poor and malnourished populations, since most GM seeds are owned and sold by powerful corporations that want to make money.

Finally, critics of transgenic foods frequently say that we simply have no business changing the genetic makeup of the fruits, vegetables, milk, juices, and meats we consume. They charge that such practices are unethical and contrary to the rules of nature. This perspective was summarized by Prince Charles, the Prince of Wales, in 1998. Writing in a London newspaper shortly before Great Britain passed a set of strong anti-GM laws, Prince Charles stated that

> I have always believed that agriculture should proceed in harmony with nature, recognizing that there are natural limits to our ambitions. . . . I happen to believe that this kind of genetic modification takes mankind into realms that belong to God, and to God alone. Apart from certain highly beneficial and specific medical applications, do we have the right to experiment with, and commercialize, the building blocks of life? We live in an age of rights—it seems to me that it is time our Creator had some rights too.[25]

A Future Filled with Superweeds and Superbugs?

Critics of GM foods claim that biotechnology companies are inadvertently creating a new generation of exceptionally strong pest species, which they nicknamed "superweeds" and "superbugs." Their argument is that when scientists with Monsanto, Dupont, and other big biotech corporations alter the genetic structure of crops to withstand pesticides, non-GM weeds and insects can gradually develop a resistance to the chemicals. At that point, farmers actually have to *increase* their use of pesticides. "Farmers who use a herbicide-tolerant [GM] crop, like RoundupReady soybeans, tend to use only the associated herbicide, like glyphosate-based Roundup, on that crop," explained environmental journalist Paul Roberts. "[This practice] causes weed populations to adapt to the herbicide and eventually become resistant to it. Once these superweeds emerge . . . farmers must find a new herbicide, and in some cases they've been switching to older, more potent products"[26] that are more harmful to the environment.

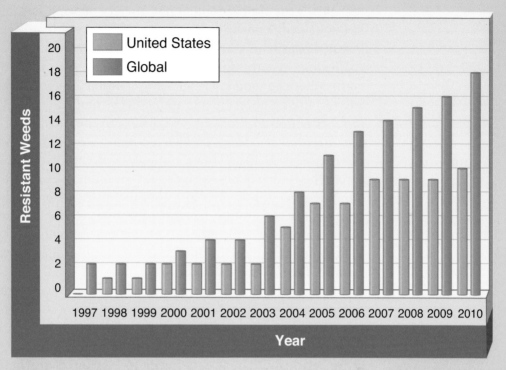

Rising Numbers of Herbicide-Resistant Weeds

As the use of GE crops resistant to RoundUp has increased, so too has the number of glyphosate-resistant weeds, both in the United States and abroad. More diverse weed management practices, for example, rotation and the use of different types of herbicides, are needed to combat this trend.

Taken from: http://insightsdels.nas.edu/?p=17.

Some scientists have warned that GM farming practices might even be creating superweeds on plots of land that are not planted with GM crops. "Pollen grains from such wind-pollinated plants as corn and canola, for instance, are carried far and wide," explained journalist J. Madeleine Nash. "Transgenic canola grown in one field, for example, can very easily pollinate nontransgenic plants grown in the next. . . . There is the possibility that as transgenes in pollen drift, they will fertilize wild plants, and weeds will emerge that are hardier and even more difficult to control."[27]

Some agricultural and environmental researchers claim that this "gene flow" problem has already become serious in the United States and other parts of the world that have invested heavily in GM technology. In 2011, for example, a coalition of twenty Indian, Southeast Asian, African, and Latin American food safety and conservation groups issued a report urging governments and biotech companies to pay more attention to the issue. According to the *Global Citizens' Report on the State of GMOs*, common weeds have now developed herbicide resistance in at least twenty-two states across the United States, with about 15 million acres (6 million hectares) of soy, corn, and cotton affected. This development, say the groups, has forced farmers to use greater quantities of deadlier herbicides to tame the resistant weeds. "The genetic engineering miracle is quite clearly faltering in farmers' fields,"[28] say the authors.

Supporters of GM crops say that these fears are exaggerated—and that farmers have been fighting stubborn weeds for centuries, anyway. Agricultural experts like Paul Pechan, however, believe that they need to take this issue more seriously. "Great care needs to be exercised when releasing GM crops into the environment because there is a danger of transgenes drifting from one plant population to another," he wrote. "This has happened in Canada with rapeseed and has led to accumulation (stacking) of various herbicide-resistant genes in one rapeseed variety."[29] Other critics have shared similar concerns. "People [in the biotech industry] should be responding to these concerns with experiments, not assurances,"[30] declared Margaret Mellon, director of the agriculture and biotechnology program for the Union of Concerned Scientists.

Opponents of GM foods also claim that if their predictions of superweeds come true, there will not be much that we can do about them. "Biological pollution will be the environmental nightmare of the twenty-first century," predicted Andrew Kimbrell, one of America's most prominent critics of GM crops. "This is not like chemical pollution—an oil

A Young Critic of Genetically Modified Foods

One of America's critics of GM foods is a young activist named Birke Baehr. Baehr became interested in sustainable farming and organic foods at age eight, when he stumbled upon some information about all the different chemicals—including dangerous toxins like mercury—that can be found in some of our processed foods. Baehr learned so much about the subject that he convinced his entire family to stop eating processed foods and start buying and growing their own organic products.

Baehr became a celebrity in sustainable farming circles in 2010, when the then eleven-year-old delivered a speech about the positive impact that organic foods can have on personal health and the environment. He delivered the speech at a special event organized by TED (Technology, Entertainment, Design), a nonprofit organization devoted to the exchange of ideas for improving the world. In his speech, Baehr recalled, "I used to think that all of our food came from these happy little farms where pigs rolled in mud and cows grazed on grass all day." When he learned about genetically modified organisms (GMOs) and chemicals in our food supply, though, he decided that he had to speak out. "Taking the DNA of a fish and putting it into the DNA of a tomato?," he told the audience. "Yuck! Don't get me wrong. I like fish and tomatoes. But this is just creepy!"

Since his highly publicized speech, Baehr has continued to speak out at events around the country on behalf of sustainable farming methods and against GM foods. He maintains his own website (www.birkeonthefarm.com) and is working on an illustrated book about his experiences called *Birke on the Farm: A Boy's Quest for Real Food.*

Birke Baehr. "What's Wrong with Our Food System? And How Can We Make a Difference?," August 28, 2010. TED.com. www.tedxnextgenerationasheville.com/.

spill—that eventually disperses. Biological pollution is an entirely different model, more like a disease. Is Monsanto going to be held legally responsible when one of its transgenes creates a superweed or resistant insect?"[31]

Ripping Holes in Natural Ecosystems

GM critics also worry that transgenic crops could harm wildlife and cause lasting damage to fragile food chains. What will happen, they ask, if GM farming practices wipe out weedy plants that some bird species rely on for survival? Or if insects that are important food sources for small mammals and birds disappear due to the introduction of pest-resistant GM plants?

Some conservationists and scientists believe that wild ecosystems are already in danger of unraveling because of the unintended consequences of GM agriculture. They frequently point to the example of the colorful monarch butterfly. The population of this beloved migratory insect has fallen dramatically since the mid-1990s. In 2011 researchers reported in the journal *Insect Conservation and Diversity* that genetically engineered corn and soybeans have been a leading factor in the decline of the monarch.

The study focused specifically on the impact of GM corn and soybeans that have been designed to withstand herbicide treatments. By 2009 herbicide-resistant corn and soybeans accounted for more than 70 percent of all U.S. production of both these crops. According to the authors of the study, farmers who use these types of seeds—usually Monsanto's RoundupReady brand of herbicide-resistant corn and soybeans—have dramatically increased their applications of glyphosate herbicides on their fields. In 2007, for example, 185 million pounds (84 million kgs) of glyphosate was applied on U.S. crops—five times as much as in 1997.

The study claims that this increase in glyphosate usage has decimated milkweed plants, which monarch butterflies rely on for essential habitat and food. "Milkweed has disappeared from at least 100 million acres of these row crops," said one of the study's coauthors. "Your milkweed is virtually gone."[32] Another researcher on insects

Conservationists claim that the monarch butterfly population has dropped because a chemical used by farmers who grow GM corn and soybeans has decimated the milkweed plant, its primary source of food.

warned that farmers' increased reliance on glyphosate herbicides threatens to become an environmental catastrophe not only for the monarch butterfly, but for other species as well. "[Glyphosate] kills everything," said entomologist Lincoln P. Brower. "It's like absolute Armageddon for biodiversity over a huge area."[33]

Accused of Contributing to Food Allergies

Health concerns about genetically modified crops also have been with us since the mid-1990s, when GM foods first began appearing in America's kitchens and grocery stores.

Scientists and consumers alike complained that the country needed to put more safeguards in place before GM foods were allowed to flood the marketplace. In 2000, for example, pediatric neurologist Martha Herbert wrote that

> the vast majority of foods in supermarkets contain genetically modified substances whose effects on our health are unknown. As a medical doctor, I can assure you that no one in the medical profession would attempt to perform experiments on human subjects without their consent. Such conduct is illegal and unethical. Yet manufacturers of genetically altered foods are exposing us to one of the largest uncontrolled experiments in modern history.[34]

A food label indicates that a product is free of wheat, dairy, and egg ingredients, which is important information for people with food allergies.

Since that time, the controversy over the long-term impact of genetically engineered foods on human health has continued. In fact, it seems to intensify with each passing year. Many of today's food safety websites and magazines are crammed with stories warning that GM foods could trigger the creation of new food allergies that could endanger the health and well-being of consumers. They describe nightmare scenarios in which a person with food allergies might eat a food he or she thinks is safe, only to fall sick because the food is actually a transgenic product that contains a protein from another plant or animal to which the person is allergic.

These complaints have received a lot of attention in recent years, especially because of strong evidence that allergy rates for nuts, shellfish, and other foods seem to be on the rise in many parts of the world where GM crops are being produced. These developments took on particular meaning to many American consumers after 2000, when authorities learned that GM corn that had only been approved for use as livestock feed had become mixed up in taco shells. This incident convinced many people that U.S. food safety laws were too loose to protect them from troublesome GM food products.

Critics also point to events such as a 2005 GM food study undertaken by the Australian government's chief science agency. The study found that a gene from a bean that had been inserted into pea plants in an effort to make them resistant to a predator insect unexpectedly triggered an allergic response when the peas were fed to test mice. Such findings, say critics, show that GM foods could accidentally expose humans to allergies as well. "When inserted, genes can get disrupted, fused, mutated, or altered in unknown ways," said Doug Gurian-Sherman, a senior scientist at the Institute for Food Safety.[35]

Defenders of GM foods, though, emphasize that numerous research studies have failed to turn up clear linkages between higher allergy rates and GM foods. They also claim that GM laboratories have established extremely sophisticated screening programs to make sure that they do not accidentally introduce new allergens into the food supply. After all, they note, the allergenic pea plants that were the focus of the Australian study never did receive approval for human consumption.

One GM Technology Giant's Controversial Business Practices

Monsanto is the best-known and most powerful company in the world of agricultural biotechnology. It is also the most controversial one. In recent years, environmental, farming, and consumer groups have all complained bitterly about the company's successful marketing of GM seeds that work only when paired with Monsanto's own Roundup herbicides. In addition, the company has gained a fearsome reputation for launching expensive lawsuits and other legal actions against small farmers, seed dealers, and dairy farms that arouse its anger.

Some of these legal actions—or attacks, in the view of critics—have swirled around Monsanto's artificial growth hormone (known as rBGH) for dairy cows. When some dairy operations that do not use rBGH began advertising their milk as "rBGH-free" in order to attract consumers who do not want to buy genetically modified milk, Monsanto filed lawsuits against them. According to Monsanto, the advertisements implied that Monsanto's growth hormone was unsafe. The dairy farmers responded that their advertisements made no claims one way or another about the safety of rBGH; they simply informed consumers that their milk was not produced with the help of rBGH.

The lid of a carton of Ben & Jerry's ice cream notes the company's position against the use of rBGH.

The majority of Monsanto's lawsuits have been filed against farmers and seed-store owners that it suspects of using the company's patented crop seeds illegally. Many farmers claim, however, that they are being unfairly persecuted by Monsanto and its "seed police"—private investigators who monitor farming practices in America's heartland. "Some farmers don't fully understand that they aren't supposed to save Monsanto's seeds for next year's planting," wrote journalists Donald Barlett and James Steele. "Still others say that they don't use Monsanto's genetically modified seeds, but seeds have been blown into their fields by wind or deposited by birds. . . . Even if a farmer doesn't buy GM seeds and doesn't want them on his land, it's a safe bet he'll get a visit from Monsanto's seed police if crops grown from GM seeds are discovered in his fields."

Donald L. Barlett and James B. Steele. "Monsanto's Harvest of Fear." *Vanity Fair,* May 2008. www.vanityfair.com/politics/features/2008/05/monsanto200805.

These assurances do not satisfy U.S. consumers like Robyn O'Brien, a mother of four who became a food safety advocate after her nine-month-old daughter nearly died from an allergic reaction to eggs. "We can't know that food allergies are caused by GMOs [genetically modified organisms] just because they both rose at the same time," she admitted. "There's a strong enough correlation, however, that I feel it merits [more] investigation."[36]

A Threat to Human Health?

Another concern raised by opponents of transgenic food is disease. A number of GM foods have been modified over the years using genes from viruses and bacteria. When these genes are introduced into target organisms, though, scientists usually attach an antibiotic-resistant "marker gene" along with the genes from the bacterium or virus. Scientists use the marker genes to conduct complicated tests that help them figure out whether the new genes have been successfully transplanted.

Foes of transgenic crops argue that these antibiotic-resistant marker genes have the potential to transfer their resistance to other bacteria that already exist in our digestive system. If that happens, we might suddenly be grappling with fearsome new disease-causing bacteria that can no longer be defeated by the usual antibiotic drugs.

The bottom line, according to GM critics, is that neither government agencies nor biotech corporations have conducted the sort of studies that might reassure consumers about the long-term safety of GM foods. Wisconsin geneticist William von Meyer points out that when the Food and Drug Administration first approved the use of bovine growth hormone (rBGH) in dairy cows back in 1993, the longest study of rBGH's safety at that time covered only a ninety-day laboratory test with small animals. Years later, food safety groups note that the U.S. government has yet to

A dairy farmer holds syringes containing rBGH, the use of which increases his cows' milk production. Some claim that testing on the health effects of rBGH on humans who drink milk was insufficient prior to the FDA's approval of its use in 1994.

undertake any long-term studies of the safety of milk from genetically modified dairy cows. "But people drink milk for a lifetime,"[37] said von Meyer.

Feeding Hungry Mouths or Filling Corporate Coffers?

Supporters of GM foods have long emphasized that the technology could help reduce rates of hunger, malnutrition, and disease in poor countries around the world. Even this argument, however, has come under fire from skeptics of transgenic technology. For one thing, GM critics say that most current transgenic food research does not really focus on improving or protecting crops that are important in the developing world. Journalist Peter Pringle points to places like Africa, where "a parasitic weed of the genus *Striga* inserts a sort of underground hypodermic needle into the roots of corn and sorghum, sucking off water and nutrients. A hundred million people on small farms in Africa lose some or all of their crops to *Striga*. A U.S biotech company developed a biotech defense for this scourge, but it never reached Africa because Africans had neither the scientific infrastructure to develop it nor the funds to pay for it."[38]

Instead, transgenic food research is mostly concerned with improving big cash crops like corn, cotton, and soy, all of which are grown in greater quantities by the United States—the wealthiest country in the world—than any other place. "The larger risk is that the transgenic industry will simply bypass the developing world altogether," wrote journalist Paul Roberts. "Not only is transgenic research missing poor-country crops . . . it is largely avoiding the traits needed by

Greenpeace activists hold a sign in front of the Monsanto headquarters in Manila, Philippines, as part of a protest over the introduction of GM corn in that country.

the developing world, especially drought and salt tolerance and resistance to tropical diseases."[39]

Other opponents argue that GM crops actually pose a threat to the citizenry in the poor countries where they have been introduced. Setting aside questions about the long-term health impact of GM crops, critics say that transgenic foods shake the foundations of third world farming communities. They charge that traditional farming practices and crop species could be lost forever in the rush to plant GM fields. "Only 150 crop species [are grown commercially worldwide], but another 7,000 play key roles in poor people's diets," wrote journalist Peter Pringle. "What will happen to all those species in a world where economic incentives increasingly favor the planting of just a handful of high-profit GM crops?"[40]

The main problem, according to many anti-GM observers, is that creating and growing GM foods is so expensive that a small number of wealthy biotech companies and farming empires basically "own" the technology. As GM crops account for an ever greater percentage of our food production, the companies that hold the patents on those crops (and the herbicides used on GM fields) grow richer and richer. "Seeds are the first link of the food chain," said Hope Shand, a food technology analyst. "And whoever controls the seeds controls the food supply. We're not talking about software or mousetraps. We're talking about the very basis of the food system, and the fact that it is in fewer and fewer hands is something that should concern everyone."[41]

Playing God

Finally, some people believe that altering the genetic structure of plants, trees, and animals for the "improvement" of our food or other purposes is simply immoral. To people like organic farming advocate Ronnie Cummins, we need to ask ourselves not only whether we *can* create GM foods, but whether we *should* create GM foods. "Gene engineers all over the world are now snipping, inserting, recombining, rearranging, editing and programming genetic material," said Cummins. "Animal genes and even human genes are randomly inserted into the chromosomes of plants, fish, and animals, creating heretofore unimaginable transgenic

Activists in Cambridge, Massachusetts, protest against the introduction of GM products into the U.S. food supply. In addition to concerns about the impact on human health and the environment, some critics see the use of GM foods as immoral and unethical.

life forms. For the first time in history, transnational bio-technology corporations are becoming the architects and 'owners' of life."[42]

Supporters of GM technology do not agree with claims that altering DNA in food to make it more nutritious or disease-resistant is unethical or unwise. They point out human history is full of advances in scientific knowledge and beneficial changes to society—many of which were harshly condemned when they were first introduced.

Many people who are uncomfortable with GM foods admit that those points are valid. Some even agree that bioengineered foods have the potential to relieve the enormous pain and suffering that goes on in many hungry corners of the globe. Nonetheless, they have profound religious and ethical doubts about whether we are using GM crops and livestock to improve nature. They express concern that we are treating the wonders of nature disrespectfully by "playing God." "If Nature has spent millions of years building a structure with natural boundaries, it must be there for a purpose," declared Dr. Michael Antonious, a British molecular geneticist. "It is there to guide the evolution of life and to maintain its integrity. Using genetic engineering in agriculture is like trying to fix something that has nothing wrong with it in the first place."[43]

Millions of Americans thus remain torn on the issue of genetically modified foods. They see the potential advantages of the science, but they worry that its use could spiral out of control. "The debate over this technology has largely centered on the science issues, but there is clearly an ethical side to it as well that is shaping American hearts and minds," summarized biotechnology expert Michael Rodemeyer. "While Americans have concerns about moving genes between different species, they also support the idea that we have been empowered by God to understand nature and use science and technology to improve the human condition."[44]

CHAPTER 5

The Future of Genetically Engineered Crops and Other Foods

Both opponents and supporters of GM foods agree that the challenge of generating enough food to feed everyone on our planet is going to get tougher in the years ahead. In 2011 the world population reached 7 billion people. Population experts expect that we will add another 2 billion people to that total within the next four decades. If we already have an estimated 800 million people going hungry every day, how can we possibly deal with the arrival of another 2 billion mouths to feed? The answer, say pro-GM scientists and policy makers, is through increased investment in bioengineering and GM crops.

Opponents claim that improvements to traditional farming practices and other antipoverty measures are the best approach to dealing with population growth. They grudgingly admit, though, that GM foods are here to stay. GM crops already have become a dominant presence in U.S. agriculture, and they have become an important part of farming policy in India and China, the most heavily populated nations on earth. The main question, then, is not *whether* GM foods will be a big part of the world's diet in the years to come. The main question surrounding GM foods is *how* these crops and products will develop and change as we march deeper into the twenty-first century.

An Age of "Frankenfish"?

Scientists have expressed great excitement about the next great advance in genetically modified foods—the introduction of bioengineered versions of salmon, pigs, and other animals that have long been consumed by humans. They claim that GM animals can help meet global food shortages, relieve fishing pressure on threatened species, and become a great source of protein (which the body uses to build muscle and organs).

These sorts of arguments do not impress people like Lindsay and Allison, though. The eleven-year-old twins believe that the risks of making GM animals outweigh the benefits. "What if [GM salmon] get out into the oceans?" asks Allison. "They'll just eat all the regular salmon and other small fish." Lindsay agrees. She believes that if people are that worried about fishing salmon and other commercially valuable fish species to extinction, "they should just make more no-fishing zones in the ocean."[45]

The worries expressed by these young girls are echoed by millions of adults—including some scientists, doctors, farm-

A member of the activist group Food and Water Watch sits behind a box containing public comments opposing the Food and Drug Administration (FDA) approval of the sale of GM salmon as she prepares to address a group of FDA advisers in September 2010.

171,645 **Public Comments** Opposing the Approval of Genetically Engineered Salmon

ers, environmental activists, and aid workers in the developing world. "What will happen to wild fish and marine species," asks organic food advocate Ronnie Cummins, "when scientists release into the environment carp, salmon, and trout that are twice as large, and eat twice as much food, as their wild counterparts?"[46]

This debate took on even greater urgency in 2011, when the U.S. government gave signals that it was on the verge of approving a type of GM salmon for sale in American grocery stores, restaurants, and fish markets. This GM salmon is called the AquAdvantage salmon. It was created by researchers at a company called AquaBounty Technologies.

AquaBounty claims that its GM salmon is nutritious, safe to eat, and tastes just as good as wild salmon. Despite these assurances, though, some food safety groups and consumers are calling on Congress to prevent GM salmon and other bioengineered animals from being approved for commercial sale. Public officials in some states have listened to these calls. In California and Alaska, for example, lawmakers have introduced bills that would permit the sale of GM salmon only if it was labeled as a genetically modified food. Meanwhile, there is a movement in Congress to prevent the U.S. Food and Drug Administration (FDA) from giving final approval of the salmon.

In light of this continued strong opposition, AquaBounty and government authorities have started working together to address the complaints of opponents. In late 2011, for example, the U.S. Department of Agriculture (USDA) awarded AquaBounty nearly half a million dollars to research ways to make the AquAdvantage salmon sterile. Rendering GM salmon sterile "would reduce the likelihood they could reproduce with wild salmon, should any escape into the wild,"[47] explained journalist Clare Leschin-Hoar.

Whatever the fate of the AquAdvantage salmon, most followers of GM technology expect that it is only a matter

---

FOOD FACT

In 2010 European Union authorities approved the cultivation of a genetically modified crop—an extra-starchy potato developed by the company BASF—for the first time since 1998.

of time until some countries begin offering meat from GM animals to consumers. They point out that researchers in laboratories around the world are already working to produce healthier, tastier, and faster-growing pigs, cows, chickens, and other livestock for the world's dinner tables.

A New Generation of GM Crops

Scientists also believe that the world may be on the verge of unveiling a new generation of genetically modified crop seeds. The first GM seeds were designed primarily to increase crop resistance to weeds and insects. Since then, however, scientists have spent more time exploring ways to create GM plants that can grow in extremely hot, cold, wet, and dry regions of the world. They are even working on creating GM seeds capable of growing in nutrient-poor soil that is unable to support conventional seeds.

GM supporters say that this research could improve—or even save—the lives of millions of people in poor parts of Africa, Asia, and Latin America. Many countries in these regions have only limited volumes of land that are suitable for raising conventional crops. In some areas the ground is too salty or acidic for crop growing. In other places long stretches of drought or flooding make it hard to farm. If scientists can engineer seeds that can grow in these types of conditions, then food production can reach levels never seen before—and longstanding problems with hunger and malnutrition might finally start to decline.

With this goal in mind, researchers all around the world are developing GM versions of traditional crops. In Asia, bioengineers in China, India, Indonesia, the Philippines, and other countries are developing GM bananas, cabbage, cassava, cauliflower, chickpeas, coffee, corn, cotton, eggplant, mangoes, melons, mustard, plantains, potatoes, rice, sugarcane, sweet potatoes, and other traditional crops. In Latin America, GM versions of bananas, beans, citrus fruits, corn, potatoes, rice, strawberries, and wheat are being introduced. In Africa, the United States, and other countries, scientists are adding genetic material to essential African foods like bananas and plantains to give them greater capacity to withstand insects and drought.[48]

A Sheep Named Dolly

Food production is not the only area of scientific research that has been revolutionized by genetic engineering. The ability to alter the genetic structure of living creatures has also given scientists the power to clone them. Cloning is a process whereby scientists take DNA from a subject—a plant or animal—and use it to make genetically identical duplicates of that subject.

The first mammal cloned from an adult cell was Dolly, a sheep that was produced by a research team in Scotland in 1996. Since then, scientists have cloned all sorts of animals, including cows, dogs, horses, goats, and rabbits. Dolly's birth, though, is still remembered as a major event. "You can almost divide science into two segments: Before Dolly and After Dolly," recalled geneticist Renee Reijo Pera. "We had a whole different way of thinking about things. We didn't think that cloning could be done at all."

The arrival of Dolly, though, also triggered fierce debates about the wisdom of this technology. Just as with GM foods, supporters of cloning say that it can be of great benefit to humankind. They point out, for example, that cloning technology could help generate vital organs for organ transplants or help researchers develop cures for horrible diseases. Cloning could also be used to preserve endangered species or even revive extinct species. Opponents, however, worry that the technology carries a high risk of being used in immoral or dangerous ways.

Dolly the sheep was the first mammal successfully cloned from an adult cell.

Agriculture experts caution, however, that an agricultural "Gene Revolution" is only part of the answer in nations that struggle to feed their people. Higher yields of crops that are bursting with additional vitamins provide only limited help to countries that lack roads or railways to transport crops to

Farmworkers in India spray pesticide on a field of GM Bt cotton. GM versions of a variety of traditional crops have been introduced in Africa, Asia, and Latin America.

market. Nor will they transform the lives of people who are controlled by corrupt political leaders or farmers who have never learned sound farming practices. "Transgenic technologies are . . . being crushed under magic-bullet expectations," said environmental journalist Paul Roberts. "Hunger is a complex social, political, economic, and ecological problem that requires social, political, economic, and ecological solutions, none of which can be genetically engineered."[49]

Agricultural experts Felicia Wu and William P. Butz expressed similar sentiments. "It is important to remember that the root cause of hunger is poverty," they wrote. "Many factors contribute to poverty, not just poor food production." Wu and Butz emphasized that transgenic foods will have a much bigger impact if they are accompanied by meaningful social and political reforms. "If the Gene Revolution is to succeed in the developing world, many of those [reforms] must be in place to ensure the long-term benefits from GM crop planting."[50]

GM Foods and Climate Change

Scientists believe that the threat of global climate changes makes GM crop research especially important. Supporters of GM agriculture argue that bioengineered foods can help us limit the severity of climate change. They claim that since GM crops require less mechanical plowing and chemical spraying than non-GM crops, they could help reduce emissions from farming of the so-called greenhouse gases that are altering our planet's climate and weather patterns.

Even so, virtually all climate scientists believe that global warming will make it even harder for developing countries to grow food in future decades. Hot and dry countries, for example, will become even hotter and drier. If these predictions come true, it will be even more important for farmers to have access to crops that can grow in challenging environmental conditions. GM advocates note, for example, that bioengineers are designing genetically altered versions of rice,

A corn crop grows in a drought simulator at a University of Missouri research farm. Scientists are exploring GM crops that can withstand environmental changes brought on by global warming.

corn, soybeans, wheat, alfalfa, and other crops that can grow in hotter, drier, or wetter conditions than non-GM seeds.

Finally, advocates of GM food claim that if we fail to make major investments in bioengineered crops now, then we will have to convert most of our remaining wilderness areas to farmland—and get used to even more stories of malnutrition and famine around the world. "There will be no silver bullet, but it is very hard to see how it would be remotely sensible to justify not using new technologies such as GM," declared Sir John Beddington, Great Britain's top scientist, in 2011. "It is unimaginable that in the next 10 to 20 years that there will not be a worsening of [food shortages] unless we take action now, and we have to include the widest possible range of solutions."[51]

Other Research Directions for GM Foods

Genetic engineering laboratories are also expanding their research into areas they have never explored before. GM research has traditionally focused on making larger and faster-growing crops. Now, though, scientists are adding genes to foods to give them other desired properties. Some foods are being modified so as to eliminate allergic reactions. Others are being adjusted so that they carry lower quantities of fat or greater loads of vitamins.

Some crops are even being engineered to provide benefits that have nothing to do with nutrition. Researchers are hard at work on developing GM foods that can carry vaccines against deadly diseases or help combat cancer. These types of crops are sometimes called "farmaceuticals." Other bioengineering laboratories are investing resources into the creation of genetically altered plants that can produce plastic-type materials as they grow. They believe that such "bioplastics" could someday provide construction materials to manufacturers around the world. Genetically modified varieties of

How America's Annual Corn Crop Is Used

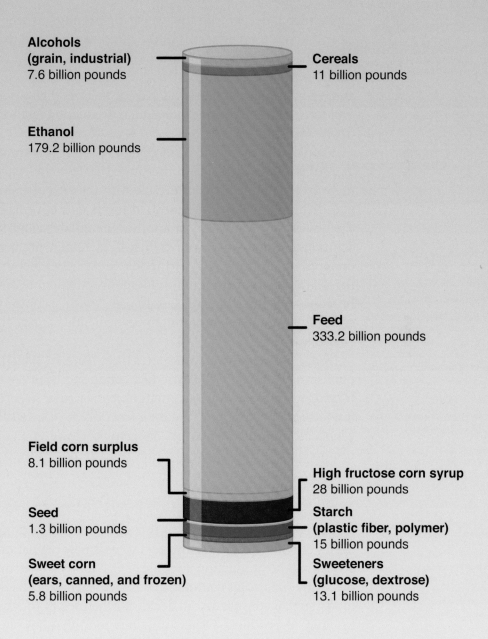

**Alcohols
(grain, industrial)**
7.6 billion pounds

Cereals
11 billion pounds

Ethanol
179.2 billion pounds

Feed
333.2 billion pounds

Field corn surplus
8.1 billion pounds

High fructose corn syrup
28 billion pounds

Seed
1.3 billion pounds

**Starch
(plastic fiber, polymer)**
15 billion pounds

**Sweet corn
(ears, canned, and frozen)**
5.8 billion pounds

**Sweeteners
(glucose, dextrose)**
13.1 billion pounds

corn, meanwhile, are already being used to produce ethanol, an alternative fuel to gasoline.

Our Future Food System

As we march deeper into the twenty-first century, it seems clear that our food system is in the midst of rapid and dramatic change. The trend toward genetic modification of the fruits, vegetables, dairy products, and meat we eat is accelerating in many parts of the world. No one believes that we will ever fully return to the traditional food production methods of our ancestors.

People hold many different opinions about this trend. Tens of millions of people in the United States and around the world are perfectly comfortable with the idea of eating and drinking genetically modified foods and beverages. They view GM foods as just another incredible scientific achievement that will improve their lives. Others are very unhappy about the rise of GM foods. Most critics feel that these Frankenfoods have not undergone sufficient testing to make sure that they are safe to eat. Another common complaint is that GM foods might permanently damage the environment.

Today's generation of kids shares these fears. In 2009 the publishing company Scholastic Inc. conducted a survey to obtain kids' views on various environmental issues. According to the Scholastic poll, the majority of kids believe that genetically modified foods are "dangerous." However, many respondents also admitted that they needed more information on GM foods before they could offer an opinion one way or the other.

Opponents of GM foods have adopted a variety of strategies to cope with the arrival of this new technology. Some critics continue to urge lawmakers to pass new regulations governing the production and sale of GM foods. For example, many Americans continue to push for labeling of all GM foods, so that consumers can decide for themselves whether to buy GM products. Others only buy food that has been produced locally by conventional farmers or through organic farming methods.

How Can You Establish a Diet Free of Genetically Modified Foods?

I t can be a challenge for American consumers to figure out whether the food they are putting in their grocery cart is genetically modified. Unlike Europe, China, Australia, Korea, Japan, and New Zealand, the United States does not require labeling of GM food. If you and your family are determined to buy non-GM food, however, there are steps you can take to keep such products off your kitchen table.

1. Buy organic. Although the United States does not require labeling of GM foods, it does maintain a certification program for organic foods. To qualify for "organic" status, foods cannot have any GM content.

2. Avoid products that contain soy, corn, cotton, or canola. The great majority of these crops raised in the United States are genetically modified. "So unless the label specifically says organic," wrote environmental journalist Jennifer Grayson, "you can pretty much bet that any food or product you buy that contains any of the big four have been genetically changed."

3. Use shopping guides produced by anti-GM groups. The Institute for Responsible Technology, for example, has produced a Non-GMO Shopping Guide that can be downloaded for free in either English or Spanish versions.

Jennifer Grayson. "Eco-Etiquette: How Can I Avoid Genetically Modified Foods?" *Huffington Post*, January 13, 2010. www.huffingtonpost.com/jennifer-grayson /eco-etiquette-how-can-i-a_b_421183.html.

In fact, the practice of organic farming—cultivating crops and livestock using natural feeds, fertilizers, and pesticides— has become a major force in the food supply system of the United States and some other countries. This so-called food movement initially arose out of fears about the health impact

Many consumers have turned to farmers markets and other sources of organic produce in order to limit their consumption of GM foods.

of consuming junk food and foods laced with pesticides and preservatives. It has gained even greater strength, though, now that GM foods have entered the food supply. "What's amazing is how quickly the food movement has become a measurable force in American society," commented *Time* in 2011. Farmers' markets and community-sponsored agriculture programs have sprung up all around the country in the last two decades, and sales of organic food and beverages jumped from $1 billion in 1990 to nearly $25 billion in 2009. In light of these trends, noted *Time*, "no less a corporate behemoth [giant] than Walmart has muscled into the organic industry, seeking out sustainable suppliers."[52]

Most observers believe, though, that organic farming will never account for more than a fraction of our total food pro-

duction. Genetically engineered food is here to stay. Given that reality, the best approach may be to make sure that this amazing technology is used safely and sensibly in the decades to come. "Like any tool, [GM foods] can be manipulated by a host of social, economic, and political forces to generate positive or negative social results," summarized scholars Pamela C. Ronald and Raoul W. Adamchak. "It seems nearly inevitable that genetic engineering will play an increasingly important role in agriculture. The question is not whether we should use [it], but more pressingly, *how* we should use it—to what responsible purpose."[53]

Chapter 1: The Development of Genetically Modified Crops

1. Quoted in Jaclyn Gallucci. "GMOs in Food: Genetically Modified Food and Our Kids," *LongIslandPress,* August 12, 2010. www.longisland press.com/2010/08/12/gmos-in -food-genetically-modified-food -and-our-kids/.
2. Gallucci. "GMOs in Food."
3. Peter Tyson. "Should We Grow GM Crops?" Harvest of Fear: A NOVA/ Frontline Special Report. PBS, 2001. www.pbs.org/wgbh/harvest /exist/.
4. Eoin O'Carroll. "Why You Should Care about Gregor Mendel," *Christian Science Monitor,* July 20, 2011. www.csmonitor.com/Innovation /2011/0720/Why-you-should-care -about-Gregor-Mendel.
5. Mark L. Winston. *Travels in the Genetically Modified Zone.* Cambridge, MA: Harvard University Press, 2002, p. 26.
6. Quoted in Marion Nestle. *Safe Food: Bacteria, Biotechnology, and Bioterrorism.* Berkeley: University of California Press, 2003, p. 198.
7. Daniel Charles. *Lords of the Harvest: Biotech, Big Money, and the Future of Food.* Cambridge, MA: Perseus, 2001, p. 145.
8. Charles. *Lords of the Harvest,* p. 149.
9. Nestle. *Safe Food,* p. 146.

Chapter 2: How Genetically Modified Foods Are Made

10. "What Is a Gene?" KidsHealth, June 2010. www.kidshealth.org/kid /talk/qa/what_is_gene.html.
11. Warren Leon and Caroline Smith DeWaal, with the Center for Science in the Public Interest. *Is Our Food Safe? A Consumer's Guide to Protecting Your Health and the Environment.* New York: Three Rivers, 2002, p. 134.
12. Leon and DeWaal. *Is Our Food Safe?,* p. 135.
13. Ian Wilmut, Keith Campbell, and Colin Tudge. *The Second Creation: Dolly and the Age of Biological Control.* New York: Farrar, Straus, and Giroux, 2000, pp. 6–7.
14. Peter Pringle. "Food, Science, and the Challenge of World Hunger: Who Will Control the Future?" *Food Inc.: A Participant Guide.* Edited by

Karl Weber. Washington, DC: Public Affairs, 2009, p. 67–68.

15. Richard Manning. "Harvest of Hope?" *OnEarth,* Winter 2005, p. 38.

16. Bernadette West, ed. *The Reporter's Environmental Handbook.* Piscataway, NJ: Rutgers University Press, 2003, p. 196.

Chapter 3: The Advantages of Genetically Modified Foods

17. Pringle. "Food, Science, and the Challenge of World Hunger," p. 71.

18. James D. Watson. *DNA: The Secret of Life.* New York: Alfred A. Knopf, 2003, pp. 150–151.

19. Johnjoe McFadden. "Fear of GM Milk Is More Science Fiction than Fact." *The Guardian (UK),* August 2, 2010. www.guardian.co .uk/commentisfree/2010/aug/02 /fear-gm-milk-science-fiction.

20. Quoted in "Harvest of Fear: Should We Grow GM Crops?" PBS, 2001. www.pbs.org/wgbh/harvest/exist /arguments.html.

21. "Global Status of Commercialized Biotech/GM Crops: 2007." ISAAA Brief 37-2007. International Service for the Acquisition of Agri-Biotech Applications, 2007. www .isaaa.org/resources/publications /briefs/37/executivesummary/.

22. Quoted in "Can Biotech Food Cure World Hunger?" Room for Debate blog. *New York Times,* October 26, 2009. www.roomfordebate.blogs

.nytimes.com/2009/10/26/can-bio tech-food-cure-world-hunger/.

23. Manning. "Harvest of Hope?," p. 38.

24. Norman Borlaug. "Billions Served." Interview with Ronald Bailey. *Reason,* April 2000. www.reason .com/archives/2000/04/01/billions -served-norman-borlaug/single page.

Chapter 4: Concerns About Genetically Modified Foods

25. His Royal Highness, Prince of Wales. "Seeds of Disaster." *Daily Telegraph (London),* June 8, 1998. www .princeofwales.gov.uk/speechesand articles/an_article_by_the_prince _of_wales_titled_the_seeds_of _disast_1857887259.html.

26. Paul Roberts. *The End of Food.* New York: Houghton Mifflin, 2008, p. 256.

27. J. Madeleine Nash. "Grains of Hope." *Time,* February 12, 2001. www .time.com/time/magazine/article /0,9171,98034,00.html.

28. Navdanya Vandana Shiva, coordinator. *The GMO Emperor Has No Clothes: A Global Citizens' Report on the State of GMOs—False Promises, Failed Technologies.* Navdanya International, 2011. www.image.guard ian.co.uk/sys-files/Environment /documents/2011/10/19/GMOEM PEROR.pdf.

29. Paul Pechan. "Basic Facts About GM Crops." *Genes on the Menu: Facts for Knowledge-Based Decisions.*

Edited by Paul Pechan and Gert E. de Vries. New York: Springer, 2005, p. 6.

30. Nash. "Grains of Hope." www.time.com/time/magazine/article/0,9171,98034,00.html.

31. Quoted in Michael Pollan. "Playing God in the Garden." *New York Times Magazine,* October 25, 1998. www.michaelpollan.com/articles-archive/playing-god-in-the-garden/.

32. Quoted in Andrew Pollack. "In Midwest, Flutters May Be Fewer." *New York Times,* July 11, 2011. www.nytimes.com/2011/07/12/science/12butterfly.html?pagewanted=all

33. Quoted in Pollack. "In Midwest, Flutters May Be Fewer." www.nytimes.com/2011/07/12/science/12butterfly.html?pagewanted=all.

34. Martha Herbert. "Genetically Altered Foods: We Are Being Exposed to One of the Largest Uncontrolled Experiments in History." *Chicago Tribune,* September 30, 2000.

35. Quoted in Starre Vartan. "Ah-Tchoo: Do Genetically Modified Foods Cause Allergies?" *E: The Environmental Magazine,* October 31, 2006. www.emagazine.com/archive/3427.

36. Quoted in Camille Chatterjee. "Is Your Kid's Food Safe? With Food Allergies and Recalls on the Rise, It's Easy to Worry About Every Bit Your Child Takes." *Redbook,* June 2009, p. 210.

37. Donald L. Barlett and James B. Steele. "Monsanto's Harvest of Fear." *Vanity Fair,* May 2008. www.vanityfair.com/politics/features/2008/05/monsanto200805.

38. Pringle. "Food, Science and the Challenge of World Hunger," p. 107.

39. Roberts. *The End of Food,* pp. 262–263.

40. Pringle. "Food, Science and the Challenge of World Hunger," p. 71.

41. Quoted in Roberts. *The End of Food,* p. 260–261.

42. Ronnie Cummins. "Hazards of Genetically Engineered Foods and Crops: Why We Need a Global Moratorium." *Food Inc.: A Participant Guide.* Edited by Karl Weber. Washington, DC: Public Affairs, 2009, p. 80.

43. Quoted in "Harvest of Fear: Should We Grow GM Crops?" PBS, 2001. www.pbs.org/wgbh/harvest/exist/arguments.html.

44. Quoted in "Views on Genetic Modification of Food Influenced by Religious Beliefs, Not Just Science." Pew Center on the States, July 26, 2001. www.pewcenteronthestates.org/news_room_detail.aspx?id=33476.

Chapter 5: The Future of Genetically Modified Crops and Other Foods

45. Interview with the author, November 21, 2011.

46. Cummins. "Hazards of Genetically Engineered Foods and Crops," p. 86.

47. Clare Leschin-Hoar. "Feds Help GMO Salmon Swim Upstream." *Grist.org,* September 29, 2011. www.grist.org/food/2011-09-29-feds-help-gmo-salmon-swim-upstream.

48. Jennifer A. Thomson. *Seeds for the Future: The Impact of Genetically Modified Crops on the Environment.* Ithaca, NY: Cornell University Press, 2007, p. 137.

49. Roberts. *The End of Food,* p. 263.

50. Felicia Wu and William P. Butz. *The Future of Genetically Modified Crops: Lessons from the Green Revolution.* Santa Monica, CA: Rand Corporation, 2004, pp. 67–68.

51. Quoted in Robin McKie. "Genetically Modified Crops are the Key to Human Survival, Says UK's Chief Scientist." *The Observer (London),* January 22, 2011. www.guardian.co.uk/environment/2011/jan/23/gm-foods-world-population-crisis.

52. Bryan Walsh. "Foodies Can Eclipse (and Save) the Green Movement." *Time,* February 15, 2011. www.time.com/time/health/article/0,8599,2049255,00.html.

53. Pamela C. Ronald and Raoul W. Adamchak. *Tomorrow's Table: Organic Farming, Genetics, and the Future of Food.* New York: Oxford University Press, 2008, pp. 166–167.

agribusiness: The wide range of industries involved in commercial food production, from farming establishments and seed sellers to manufacturers of farming equipment.

bioengineering: Using engineering techniques and principles to work with, study, and make changes to living organisms.

biotech: A shortened version of the term *biotechnology*.

biotechnology: Modifying the genetic structure of living organisms to make new commercial products (like pest-resistant crops). Also sometimes known as genetic modification and genetic engineering.

conventional farming: Raising crops or livestock without using genetic modification (GM) technology.

genetics: The science of studying the cellular structure of all living things, with a special emphasis on how traits are passed on from generation to generation through heredity.

GM: Genetically modified.

GMO: Genetically modified organism.

herbicide: A type of pesticide used specifically to kill weeds or other undesirable plants.

heredity: The transmission of genes from one generation of an organism to the next.

organic foods: Foods that are raised and sold without using man-made preservatives or chemicals (such as synthetic fertilizers or herbicides).

patent: Legal recognition given to the creator of an invention to make, use, or sell that invention exclusively for a given period of time.

pesticide: A chemical used to kill insects, weeds, and other pests.

traits: Characteristics.

transgenic: Genetically modified.

yield: The full amount or volume of a crop or other agricultural product.

AgBioWorld Foundation

PO Box 85
Tuskegee Institute
AL 36087
(334) 444-7884
www.agbioworld.org

This nonprofit organization maintains a well-known website that provides information on agricultural biotechnology issues around the world. Both the organization and the website are overseen by C.S. Prakash, who is a recognized authority on—and supporter of—genetically modified food production.

Alliance for Better Foods

700 13th St. NW, Ste. 800
Washington, DC 20005
(202) 783-4573
www.betterfoods.org

The Alliance for Better Foods is a public relations effort supported by a wide range of corporations and interest groups that are involved in the production or sale of genetically modified foods in the United States. The organization's website provides a wide range of information in support of bioengineered foods.

Biotechnology Industry Organization (BIO)

1201 Maryland Ave. SW, Ste. 900
Washington, DC 20024
(202) 962-9200
www.bio.org

BIO describes itself as the world's largest biotechnology organization, with more than eleven hundred members around the globe. These members range from life sciences corporations to academic institutions and regional biotech associations. BIO's mission is to educate the public about the benefits of GM foods and other bioengineering efforts and to encourage the development of policies that support transgenic technology.

Center for Food Safety

660 Pennsylvania Ave. SE, Ste. 302
Washington, DC 20003
(202) 547-9359
www.centerforfoodsafety.org

The Center for Food Safety describes itself as a nonprofit organization devoted to protecting human health and the environment by opposing genetically modified food and other "harmful" food production technologies. The center is an advocate for organic food production and other sustainable forms of agriculture.

Consumers Union

101 Truman Ave.
Yonkers, NY 10703
(914) 378-2000
www.consumersunion.org

Consumers Union is a nonprofit organization that works on behalf of consumers to ensure that they can make informed purchasing decisions. The group is best known for its magazine *Consumer Reports,* which tests the quality of all manner of consumer products ranging from automobiles to MP3 players. The organization maintains a number of divisions, though, including one devoted to food safety. Consumers Union has issued repeated calls for better labeling and safety testing of GM foods sold in the United States.

Organic Consumers Association (OCA)

6771 South Silver Hill Dr.
Finland, MN 55603
(218) 226-4164
www.organicconsumers.org

The OCA is one of America's leading advocacy organizations for organic food production. The OCA and its 1 million members and volunteers are also prominent critics of GM foods. The group's website features extensive coverage of GM food issues and provides interested parties with information on grassroots efforts to stop GM foods and promote organic foods.

Sierra Club

85 Second St., 2nd Fl.
San Francisco, CA 94105
(415) 977-5500
www.sierraclub.org

The Sierra Club is America's largest environmental protection and wilderness conservation organization. Its website provides a good overview of environmental concerns that have been raised about genetically modified food production.

Books

Jerri Freedman. *Genetically Modified Food: How Biotechnology Is Changing What We Eat.* New York: Rosen, 2009. Provides an overview of the history and science of genetically modified foods.

Lauri S. Friedman. *Genetically Modified Foods.* Farmington Hills, MI: Lucent, 2008. This book provides a variety of perspectives on the safety and usefulness of genetically modified foods. Both critics and supporters of GM foods weigh in on issues ranging from the environmental impact of GM crops to the technology's value in addressing worldwide hunger and malnutrition.

Andrew Kimbrell. *Your Right to Know: Genetic Engineering and the Secret Changes in Your Food.* San Rafael, CA: Earth Aware, 2007. Written by the director of the Center for Food Safety, a leading anti-GM food organization. This book lays out all the main arguments against GM foods. It also includes a fourteen-page guide to buying non-GM foods at your local supermarket.

Peter Pringle. *Food Inc.: Mendel to Monsanto—The Promises and Per-*

ils of the Biotech Harvest. New York: Simon and Schuster, 2005. A fine overview of the controversy over GM foods for high-level readers. The author explains all the different debates surrounding GM foods in clear and understandable language— and concludes that both critics and supporters of the technology have lots of support for their positions.

Martin Tietel and Kimberly Ann Wilson. *Genetically Engineered Food: Changing the Nature of Nature.* Rochester, VT: Park Street, 2001. Provides a clear rundown of the various arguments that people have made against GM foods, including their alleged danger to the environment and human health.

Websites

AgBioSafety (www.agbiosafety.unl .edu). A University of Nebraska– Lincoln website that aims to be the premier source for scientific and educational information on the debate over genetically modified foods.

Council for Biotechnology Information (www.whybiotech.com). Includes a wide range of information about the benefits and safety of agricultural biotechnology and its contributions to sustainable agricultural development in the United States and around the world. Members of the CBI include Monsanto, Du Pont, and other leading biotechnology companies across the globe.

GM Organisms (www.newscientist.com /topic/gm-food). Wide-ranging coverage of GM food and other genetic engineering issues from *New Scientist,* which explores and explains science issues and discoveries in accessible and entertaining ways.

Harvest of Fear: Exploring the Growing Fight over Genetically Modified Food (www.pbs.org/wgbh/harvest/). This is a companion website to a PBS/Frontline television special that was broadcast in 2001. It includes a wide range of information on GM foods, including a "Should We Grow GM Crops?" section that provides understandable explanations of all the arguments for and against transgenic foods.

Non-GMO Project (www.nongmopro ject.org). A website dedicated to providing support and encouragement to consumers and organizations who want to have non-GM food alternatives.

Non-GMO Shopping Guide (www .nongmoshoppingguide.com). Maintained by the Institute for Responsible Technology, this website provides shoppers with tips for avoiding genetically modified foods. The website also includes downloadable shopping guides (in both English and Spanish) that include a listing of more than 150 store brands that do not use GM ingredients in their products.

INDEX

A

Adamchak, Raoul W., 48, 79
Agribusiness, rise of, 15–17
Allergies, GM foods may increase, 58–59, 61
Animals, bioengineered, 68–70
Anther culture, 29
Antonious, Michael, 66
AquaBounty Technologies, 69
Athletic ability, use of genes to predict, 30
Atlas Sports Genetics, 30

B

Bacillus thuringiensis (Bt), 35
Baehr, Birke, 55
Bartlett, Donald, 60
Beddington, John, 74
Biolistics, 31–32
Bioplastics, 74
Borlaug, Norman, 49–50
Brinjal (vegetable), *46*
Brower, Lincoln P., 57
Bt (*Bacillus thuringiensis*), 35

C

Calcium phosphate precipitation, 32

Calgene, 19, 20
Campbell, Keith, 28
Certificate of Protection (COP), 17
Charles (Prince of Wales), 52
Charles, Daniel, 21
Chromosomes, 28
Climate change, GM foods and, 73–74
COP (Certificate of Protection), 17
Corn
    Bt, 35
    GM, *23, 73*
    RoundupReady, 56
    uses of U.S. crop, *75*
Cotton, Bt, 35, *35, 72*
Crick, Francis, 16, 26
Crops, transgenic
    amount of farmland devoted to, 25
    beneficial aspects of, 38
    Bt and HT genes in, 35
    can contaminate nontransgenetic plant nearby, 53–55
    environmental benefits of, 47, 49–50
    environmental risks of, 56–57
    global area of, *24*
    percent crafted to resist herbicides, 61
    research on, 63–64

Cross-breeding, 12
Cummins, Ronnie, 64, 69

D

Darwin, Charles, 13
deoxyribonucleic acid. *See* DNA
Department of Agriculture, U.S.
   (USDA), 22, 42
Developing nations
   do not benefit from GM crops,
     62–64
   may benefit from GM crops, 44,
     45–47, 70
DeWaal, Caroline Smith, 28
Diamond v. Chakrabarty (1980),
   17–18
DNA (deoxyribonucleic acid), *16*
   discovery of structure of, 16–17
   research on, 26–28
   techniques to manipulate, 31–34,
     33
Dolly the sheep, 71, *71*

E

Electroporation, 32
Environmental Protection Agency
   (EPA), 42
European Union (EU), 69

F

FAO (UN Food and Agriculture
   Organization), 45
Farmaceuticals, 74
Farmers' markets, 78, *78*

FDA. *See* Food and Drug
   Administration, U.S.
FlavrSavr tomato, 20–21
Food allergies, GM foods may
   increase, 58–59, 61
Food and Agriculture Organization,
   UN (FAO), 45
Food and Drug Administration, U.S.
   (FDA), 42, 56
   approval of rBGH in dairy cows,
     61

G

Gallucci, Jaclyn, 11
GE. *See* Genetic engineering
Gene marker selection, 31
Gene silencing, 34
Gene splicing, 34
Genetic engineering (GE)/gene
   transference, 8
   early work in, 27–28
   Hawaiian papaya crop saved by,
     48
   moral objections to, 64–66
   research directions for, 74–75
   as source of distrust, 34, 36–37
   techniques for, 31–34, *33*
Genetic modification, in nature, 12
Genetically modified (GM) foods, 8
   concerns of critics of, 51–52
   countries banning, 23–24
   FDA grants approval of, 18
   first arrival in U.S. groceries, 18,
     20
   U.S. agencies responsible for
     safety of, 42

U.S. food industry transformed by, 21–25
ways to avoid, 77
Genetically modified organisms (GMOs), 28
Global Citizens' Report on the State of GMOs, 54
Glyphosate, 53, 56, 57
GM foods. *See* Genetically modified foods
Green Peace, 51
Green Revolution, 49–50
Gurian-Sherman, Doug, 59

H

Herbert, Martha, 58
Herbicides
    GM crops tolerant of, 22, 35
    percent of GM crops crafted to resist, 61
    weeds resistant to, increase in, 52–54, *53*
    See also Roundup/RoundupReady crops
HT (herbicide tolerant) genes, 35
Humans/human body
    number of cells in, 32
    number of chromosomes in, 28
Hunger/malnutrition, 45–47
    global, extent of, 45
    potential of GM foods to reduce, 38, 39–40, 44

I

Insect Conservation and Diversity (journal), 56

International Food Information Council, 12

K

Kessler, David, 18
KidsHealth (website), 26
Kimbrell, Andrew, 54–55

L

Labels/labeling, 9, 19, 76
    indicating product free of wheat/dairy/egg ingredients, *58*
    of milk from rBGH-treated cows, 18
Leon, Warren, 28
Leschin-Hoar, Clare, 69
Lipofection, 32–33

M

Manning, Richard, 34
Mellon, Margaret, 54
Mendel, Gregor, 13, 14, *14,* 15
Microinjection, 33–34
Milk, from rBGH-treated cows
    FDA approval of, 18
    lack of safety testing on, 61–62
    protest of, *20*
Milkweed, glyphosate has decimated, 56
Monarch butterfly, 56–57, *57*
Monsanto Corporation, 18, 22, 35
    controversial business practices of, 60

percent of GE seed patents held by, 74

protest of, *63*

N

Nash, J. Madeleine, 53

Natural selection, 13

NOVA (TV program), 12

O

O'Brien, Robyn, 61

O'Carroll, Eoin, 13, 15

Omega-3 acids, soybeans elevating blood levels of, *39*, 39–40

Opinion polls. *See* Surveys

Organic foods

    farming, 77

    prohibition of GM ingredients, 56

    sales of, 78

P

Papaya, *48*

    genetic modification aided, 48

Pera, Renee Reijo, 71

Pesticides

    GM crops crafted with resistance to, 22

    GM crops reduce need for, 35, 38, 40, 42, 49

Plant Variety Protection Act (PVPA, 1970), 17

Polls. *See* Surveys

Population, global, 67

Pringle, Peter, 39, 62, 64

Processed food, prevalence of GM ingredients in, 22

R

rBGH (recombinant bovine growth hormone), 17

Recombinant DNA technique, 31

Roberts, Paul, 52, 63

Rodemeyer, Michael, 66

Ronald, Pamela C., 48, 79

Roth, Stephen M., 30

Roundup/RoundupReady crops, 22, 52

S

Salmon, genetically modified, 68–70

Scholastic Inc., 76

Seeds

    early hybridization of, 12–13

    patenting of, 17–18

Shand, Hope, 64

StarLink corn, 24–25

Steele, James, 60

Striga (weed species), 62

Surveys

    of children on GM foods, 76

    of number who have eaten GM foods, 22

    on GM foods, 12

T

Time (magazine), 78

Tissue culture, 29

    cauliflower grown in, *29*

Transgenes, 28

U

USDA (U.S. Department of Agriculture),
22, 42

V

Viral/bacterial carriers, 31

Von Meyer, William, 61, 62

W

Wambugu, Florence, 44
Watson, James, 16, 26, 40
Weeds, herbicide-resistant, 52–54,
53
Wilmit, Ian, 28
Winston, Mark L., 15–16

PICTURE CREDITS

Kevin Hillstrom is an independent scholar who has written extensively on health and environmental issues. His works include *U.S. Health Policy and Politics: A Documentary History* (2011).